ROUTLEDGE LIBRARY EDITIONS:
LIBRARY AND INFORMATION SCIENCE

Volume 48

INNOVATIONS IN PLANNING FACILITIES FOR SCI-TECH LIBRARIES

INNOVATIONS IN PLANNING FACILITIES FOR SCI-TECH LIBRARIES

Edited by
ELLIS MOUNT

LONDON AND NEW YORK

First published in 1986 by The Haworth Press, Inc.

This edition first published in 2020
by Routledge
2 Park Square, Milton Park, Abingdon, Oxon OX14 4RN

and by Routledge
52 Vanderbilt Avenue, New York, NY 10017

Routledge is an imprint of the Taylor & Francis Group, an informa business

© 1986 The Haworth Press, Inc.

All rights reserved. No part of this book may be reprinted or reproduced or utilised in any form or by any electronic, mechanical, or other means, now known or hereafter invented, including photocopying and recording, or in any information storage or retrieval system, without permission in writing from the publishers.

Trademark notice: Product or corporate names may be trademarks or registered trademarks, and are used only for identification and explanation without intent to infringe.

British Library Cataloguing in Publication Data
A catalogue record for this book is available from the British Library

ISBN: 978-0-367-34616-4 (Set)
ISBN: 978-0-429-34352-0 (Set) (ebk)
ISBN: 978-0-367-36309-3 (Volume 48) (hbk)
ISBN: 978-0-367-36311-6 (Volume 48) (pbk)
ISBN: 978-0-429-34522-7 (Volume 48) (ebk)

Publisher's Note
The publisher has gone to great lengths to ensure the quality of this reprint but points out that some imperfections in the original copies may be apparent.

Disclaimer
The publisher has made every effort to trace copyright holders and would welcome correspondence from those they have been unable to trace.

Innovations in Planning Facilities for Sci-Tech Libraries

Ellis Mount, Editor

The Haworth Press
New York • London

Innovations in Planning Facilities for Sci-Tech Libraries has also been published as *Science & Technology Libraries*, Volume 7, Number 1, Fall 1986.

© 1986 by The Haworth Press, Inc. All rights reserved. No part of this book may be reproduced or utilized in any form or by any means, electronic or mechanical, including photocopying, microfilm and recording, or by any information storage and retrieval system, without permission in writing from the publisher. Printed in the United States of America.

The Haworth Press, Inc., 12 West 32 Street, New York, NY 10001
EUROSPAN/Haworth, 3 Henrietta Street, London WC2E 8LU England

Library of Congress Cataloging in Publication Data

Innovations in planning facilities for sci-tech libraries.

"Has also been published as Science & technology libraries, volume 7, number 1, fall 1986"—T.p. verso.
  1. Scientific libraries—United States—Planning. 2. Technical libraries—United States—Planning. I. Mount, Ellis.
Z675.T3I48 1986   026.5   86-14849
ISBN 0-86656-592-2

Innovations in Planning Facilities for Sci-Tech Libraries

Science & Technology Libraries
Volume 7, Number 1

CONTENTS

Introduction	1
Creating a New Library Facility for Ayerst Laboratories Research, Inc.	3
Barbara Boyajian	
Introduction	3
Planning the Library	4
Moving the Collection	6
The New Facility	8
Establishing the New Library	9
Conclusion	10
Statistics	11
A New Pharmaceutical Company Library: The Upjohn Company Corporate Technical Library	15
Lorraine Schulte	
Library Services	16
Library Collection	17
Library Systems	17
Old Facility	18
Purpose of the New Facility	18
Planning	19
Design Requirements and Building Constraints	20

The New Library	21
Special Features	23
Outcome	26
Statistics	27

The John Crerar Library of the University of Chicago 31
Patricia K. Swanson

History and Background	31
The Move	33
The Mission of the New Library	34
Service Concepts Underlying the Design of the New Library	35
Description of the Facility	36
Problems in the New Library	37
The Future of a Centralized Science Library	38
Statistics	39

The New O'Callahan Science Library at the College of the Holy Cross 45
Tony Stankus

Motivation	45
Assembling the Team	47
Identifying Major Goals	47
The Results—Left Wing	48
The Results—Right Wing	50
Customer Relations	51
Options for the Future	51
Summary of Features	51

The Libraries of the Los Alamos National Laboratory 57
Lois Erwin Godfrey

Description of the Library System	57
The Facility for the Main and Report Libraries: The J. Robert Oppenheimer Study Center	58
Planning for the Facility	59
Layout and Features	60
Compromises, and Post-Occupancy Changes	61
Hindsight	62
Statistics	63

SPECIAL PAPER

Impact of Online Search Services on Special Libraries   67
Pamela G. Kobelski
Betty Miller

Introduction	68
Survey	68
Library Data	68
Online Searching	72
Online Searching and Print Subscriptions	76
Overall Effects on Special Libraries	79
Summary of Survey Results	80
Bibliography	80

SCI-TECH COLLECTIONS   87
Tony Stankus, Editor

Information Sources in Laser Science and Technology   89
Emerson Hilker

Background	89
Future Developments	92
Laser Literature	94
Research Reports and Patents	97
Monographs and Monographic Series	98
Bibliographies	101
Abstracting and Indexing Services	103
Organizations	107

NEW REFERENCE WORKS IN SCIENCE AND TECHNOLOGY   111
Robert G. Krupp, Editor

SCI-TECH ONLINE   151
Ellen Nagle, Editor

National Online Meeting	151
Database News	152
Search System News	155
Publications and Search Aids	155

SCI-TECH IN REVIEW   157
Karla Pearce and
Giuliana Lavendel, Editors

Introduction

Many of our readers may recall that this journal devoted an earlier issue (Summer 1983) to the topic of planning facilities for sci-tech libraries. Evidence from a number of readers indicated that the issue was helpful to them. Since the creation of sci-tech libraries continues each year, it was felt that another issue on this topic after the passage of a little more than three years would be worth having.

This issue contains descriptions of five facilities, each having unique features. The first, by Barbara Boyajian, relates the problems of designing a facility from a site in another country, a library which turned out to serve well the scientists of Ayerst Laboratories. Another corporate research center, that of the Upjohn company, is described in the paper by Lorraine Schulte. Her account includes a lot of emphasis on the problems of designing a library that would have a very strong set of computer facilities for its users.

Academic libraries are discussed in two papers, the first being an account of the new home for the venerable John Crerar Library, which moved to the University of Chicago campus; the paper, by Patricia K. Swanson, describes the facilities as well as the problems of merging large collections. The new science library at the College of the Holy Cross, in the paper written by Tony Stankus, is shown to have a variety of study areas for users as well as a blending of conventional and mobile bookstacks.

A library serving an important government research center is described in the paper by Lois Godfrey, who has written about the main library at the busy Los Alamos National Laboratory. Although this library was designed several years ago, it is nevertheless of great interest because it is one of a few sci-tech libraries to rely heavily on solar heating; it obtains about 94% of its heat and 70% of its cooling needs from its solar collector system, surely a fact that warrants general awareness by librarians.

© 1986 by The Haworth Press, Inc. All rights reserved.

Two more library facility papers will be found in Volume 7, Number 2 of this journal.

The special paper for this issue is an account by Pamela Kobelski and Betty Miller of a survey made of nearly 200 librarians in New York State about their use of online databases, including effects on printed index subscriptions.

This issue's collection development paper, prepared by Emerson Hilker, is devoted to information sources on laser science and technology, a topic of great current interest.

Our regular features conclude the issue. The *Sci-Tech Review* section is edited for the first time by its new editors, Karla J. Pearce and Giuliana Lavendel. We want to add a word of appreciation for the work done by its former editor, Suzanne Fedunok, who has found the press of duties too much for her to continue with this feature.

Ellis Mount
Editor

Creating a New Library Facility for Ayerst Laboratories Research, Inc.

Barbara Boyajian

ABSTRACT. The Ayerst Laboratories Research Library was relocated from Montreal, Canada to Ayerst's new research center in Princeton, New Jersey. The author describes the history, planning, move, and establishment of the new library facility. Special problems relating to a long distance move and the creation of library services are discussed.

INTRODUCTION

Ayerst Laboratories, originally Ayerst, McKenna and Harrison, Ltd., a Canadian pharmaceutical company, was established in 1925 in Montreal. As its product line increased, a demand for Ayerst pharmaceuticals was created beyond the Canadian border, and in 1934 a United States branch was established in Rouses Point, New York. In 1943 Ayerst, McKenna and Harrison, Ltd., was acquired by American Home Products Corporation, a diversified manufacturer and marketer of pharmaceuticals and consumer products throughout the world. Following the acquisition, Ayerst's first modern research and development laboratories were constructed in Montreal in 1944 and then significantly expanded in 1958 and 1966. Also, Ayerst's executive offices and world headquarters were established in New York City. During the next 40 years Ayerst experienced rapid growth and expansion and

---

Barbara Boyajian is the Librarian, Research Library, Ayerst Laboratories Research, Inc., CN 8000, Princeton, NJ 08540. She holds a BA degree from Albright College and a MSLS degree from Villanova University. The author wishes to thank Dr. Yvon Lefebvre, the Director of the Information Department, for background information.

© 1986 by The Haworth Press, Inc. All rights reserved.

foresaw the need for a successful research program requiring expansion of the R&D facilities beyond the confines of the Montreal site. Thus in June of 1982 it was announced that Ayerst would relocate its research efforts to a new center to be built in the Princeton area of New Jersey. Construction of a 285,000 square foot complex to house the latest in research equipment and facilities began in the fall of 1982 on a 180 acre site. The relocation decision necessitated moving an established library collection from Montreal to Princeton and required the design, planning, and implementation of a new full-service library.

PLANNING THE LIBRARY

The planning and design of the new library was carried out from Montreal by the Director of the Information Department working together with one of the Princeton-based architects for the complex.

In October 1982 a blueprint showing the location and size of the new library was sent by the architects to Montreal, and the planning process began. The new library was to be located in the east wing of the research facility and would occupy approximately 6,000 square feet, including work area and offices. The east wing was to be one story tall, so that no laboratory space would be above the library and the chances of damage from accidents eliminated. As an additional safety feature, the two inside walls of the library would be constructed as fire walls. One outside wall of the library would contain floor-to-ceiling windows and afford a bright and pleasant atmosphere. The other outside wall would be constructed to allow for an extension of the library.

A major portion of the planning consisted of establishing the amount of shelf space needed to house the existing collection, which would be moved from Montreal, and estimating the amount of additional space required for future growth. From these requirements, a functional floor plan was designed. As part of the planning process the Information Director visited several libraries in the Montreal area and made a trip to Philadelphia, Pennsylvania, to visit the newly completed library of Wyeth Laboratories, another division of

American Home Products Corporation. Through these visits he picked up pointers on layout and types of shelving and furniture, lighting, and special features which would enhance the library.

The actual floor plan was developed during the next several months. The amount of shelf space was calculated and the size of the stacks determined. These requirements were then put on paper, and through trial and error a final plan was drawn up. The floor plan and requirements were then sent back to the architect in Princeton. Upon review, the architect returned the plans expressing several objections. He had removed the shelving placed along two walls because he felt it would not be aesthetically pleasing. He also changed the lighting over the stacks to run parallel rather than perpendicularly to the aisles. The location and height of the display shelving was also changed. The architect had lowered these stacks to 42" in height. A long-distance debate now commenced. The Information Director argued that removing the wall shelving and lowering the display stacks would greatly reduce the amount of shelf space, making it no longer adequate. Also a change in the lighting would make it difficult to rearrange the shelving if the library were expanded, which was a distinct future possibility. The shelving along the walls was finally restored, but some other problems remained unsettled.

In August of 1983, the Director of the Information Department went to Princeton to meet in person with the architect. After discussing the problems, the height of the display shelving was raised to 78", but the lighting over the stacks remained parallel to the aisles. Also, several other small changes were made in the layout. Another meeting was held in the fall of 1983 to discuss the furniture and shelving. The architect had chosen these items through the presentation and bid process. They were acceptable and would fit in well with the style of the entire building. All the desks, chairs, and cabinets used in the library would be the same as those used throughout the building. Specifications were then drawn up, and the order was placed.

The final step necessary to prepare for the new library was the hiring of a librarian for the facility. The author was hired and began work on February 1, 1984. At this point, the building was still under construction and being completed in sections, with the library itself not scheduled to be finished for a few months. The delay allowed the librarian time to plan for the opening of the library, establish some library services, order supplies and equipment, and hire a staff.

MOVING THE COLLECTION

The next step in the relocation process was the packing of the books, journals, files, and equipment in Montreal for transfer to the Princeton facility. A professional moving company contracted to move the entire Research Division also packed and moved the library collection. Packing was begun during the last week of January, 1984. It was anticipated at this time that there would be a need to establish a temporary library because the actual library would not be completed for a few months. With this in mind, the packing was done in two stages. First, the current journal issues and their corresponding volumes dating back six years were packed and labeled. Then all the remaining journals and books were packed and labeled. Color-coded labels were used to differentiate between the two collections. Documents and reports were also packed along with microfilm, a microfilm reader-printer, and a photocopy machine. When finished, the entire collection occupied over 900 cartons and filled three moving vans. The vans set off from Montreal to Princeton with a stop at the Canadian-U.S. border to undergo customs inspection. They finally arrived in Princeton on February 29, 1984.

While the collection was in transit, plans were made for the temporary library to be housed in what would eventually become a conference room. Industrial shelving, which would later be used in a chemical stock room, was set up to hold the journals, and some desks, chairs, and a large table were placed in the room.

By the time the collection arrived, it was decided that professional help would be needed to do the unpacking. A library service agency with experience in moving libraries was contracted to do the job. The cartons that were to be unpacked at this time were sorted out, and the partial unpacking was completed in a few days. On March 6th the temporary library was opened for use. The current journal issues, which had already been arriving in Princeton, were opened, checked in, and placed on the shelves. The microfilm collection of journals and patents was unpacked, and the microfilm reader-printer was set up. Also, the photocopy machine was unpacked and serviced. At this point all that was offered was a basic reading room, which was adequate at best. The floor was bare concrete, and the lighting poor, since it was not designed to coordinate with the shelving.

In the meantime construction was progressing on the new library. By mid-April the electrical work was finished, the lighting and ceiling were in place, and the carpeting had been laid. Everything was now ready for the shelving, which was delivered and installed at this time. In preparation for this step, the journal collection was analyzed to determine the amount of shelf space needed for each title, allowing space for growth. The shelves were then marked, indicating where each title would begin. The company that had unpacked the temporary library was again hired to unpack the remaining cartons and move the temporary library into the new facility. The final unpacking and consolidation of the collection took eight workers five working days to complete.

The unpacking and shelving of the journals and books was not accomplished without some problems. The cartons holding the collection had been moved so many times that they were no longer in any order. Efforts were made to sort them alphabetically, but this was difficult given the sheer number. They looked like a small mountain piled in front of the library. It was also necessary to find all cartons containing a single journal title at the same time so that they could be shelved in fairly good order. It was felt that this was important to do while the movers were on the job, because there would be no personnel to do it later. Coordination of effort was essential. Some movers searched out the journals, others shelved, and the rest moved the journals from the temporary library to the new.

After everything was unpacked and shelved and the empty cartons removed, the library furniture was put into place, and the library was ready to open.

THE NEW FACILITY

The New Research Library officially opened on May 15, 1984. Its greater than 6,000 square foot space provides a pleasant atmosphere for the scientists to do their reading and reference work and for the library staff to work. The color scheme consists of beige carpeting (installed as carpet squares which can be easily replaced in case of spots or stains), off-white walls, light oak furniture, and seating upholstered in shades of maroon and wine. A number of large potted plants are placed throughout the library. The shelving is beige steel with oak end panels to match the furniture.

The journal shelving consists of eight double-faced ranges 24' long, 90" high, with 6 adjustable 10" shelves per face. Also, one single-faced range 66' long and one 33' long, both 102" high along the back walls of the library. These consist of 7 adjustable 10 inch shelves per face. The ranges all have steel canopy tops and sliding reference shelves spaced periodically throughout. The sliding shelves are very useful for the patrons, but reduce the height of the shelf below and prevent the upright shelving of most journals on those shelves. Also, the canopies, while neat in appearance, prevent adjustment of the shelves to allow all the volumes to be shelved upright. One shelf in each section of the abstracts and indexes area had to be removed so these large volumes could be shelved properly.

The book shelving consists of one double-faced range 36' long and 78" high with 5 adjustable 10" shelves per face and canopy top. No problem was encountered with shelving the book collection. The height between shelves was adequate. Another range of shelving located under the windows of the workroom was designated to hold the reference collection. This section is 33' long, 35" high, and contains one 12" adjustable shelf per face. It also has a continuous oak top to form a work space where the reference books can be placed for use.

The final range of shelving is for the current periodicals and consists of hinged sloping display shelves with flat storage shelves underneath. The section is 30' long and 78" high double-faced, with five shelves per face and a canopy top. Having the storage shelf hidden behind the sloping shelf provides a neat way to store back issues; however, it is sometimes awkward to lift up the shelf and retrieve the issue needed underneath.

The study carrels and tables are arranged throughout the library. They are all solid oak with formica tops. The card catalog and circulation desk are of the same design, and all came from the same library furniture manufacturer. The pieces for the circulation desk were chosen from a catalog and have since been modified to provide more work space. There is also a small lounge area to one side by the windows consisting of several comfortable chairs and coffee tables.

The microfilm collection and the reader-printers are housed in a separate room off the entrance to the library. The two photocopy machines are also located here. The second, larger, photocopy machine housed with the microfilm was acquired after the library opened.

The workroom and offices house the librarian and her staff along with several of the information scientists who perform literature searches. One office was designated as the terminal room and houses one terminal with modem and one IBM PC which is used for literature searching and some word processing. There is also a sink and cabinet area used to store supplies. The wall between the workroom and library consists of glass windows and affords an excellent view of the library. This allows the staff to see what is happening outside and also allows the patrons easy access to the staff.

ESTABLISHING THE NEW LIBRARY

Planning and moving the collection were only part of the process of creating the new library. It was also necessary to hire a staff, establish services, and provide the kind of resource materials necessary for the researchers at the new location.

As soon as it was known that the temporary library would be a reality, interviewing began for the staff positions. One clerk was hired and began work in April of 1984. The rest of the staff was hired and began work after the new library was opened and there was adequate work space. The assistant librarian started at the end of May and the other clerk in June. In 1985 an additional clerk was hired, bringing the staff to two professionals and three clerks.

The move from Montreal to Princeton also made it necessary to initiate new agreements with vendors to provide basic library services. Arrangements were made with local libraries and networks and commercial vendors for interlibrary loan service. A book jobber was chosen; another vendor was found for standing orders, and a binder was also chosen. The librarian's personal experience and input from other librarians in the area served as criteria for these decisions.

Another necessity for any library is supplies. Such things as interlibrary loan forms, book order forms, rubber stamps, book trucks, step stools, and other basic supplies had to be ordered. We also needed a Kardex cabinet to hold the journal check-in cards that came from Montreal, and a microfiche reader for the fiche holdings of the various library networks to which we would now have access. The best way to come up with a list of items needed is to page through any library supply catalog and to rely on past experiences.

The final objective of the new library was to provide the services and materials needed by our new research staff. During 1984 the staff increased rapidly in size, with new scientists being hired from many parts of the country. Also new research projects were being added in subject areas in which the library collection was inadequate. Over the past two years, over fifty new journal titles have been added, and the book collection is also being expanded.

CONCLUSION

The Ayerst Research Library has now been open for over a year and a half. It has been well received by the research staff and is used regularly. On the whole it is very bright and spacious, and the layout works wells for the library staff and patrons.

This account of the planning and move of one library should not be used as a model for others, because each library is faced with its own unique set of circumstances. It is important to be flexible, but have an overall schedule and list of things to be accomplished, to use the professionals made available to you, and to seek input from peers who have completed a successful move themselves.

STATISTICS

Gross area	6,000 sq. ft.
Staff size	
Professional	2
Non-Professional	3
Seating for users	36
Employees served at location	
Current	320
Anticipated	500
Collection size	
Books	4,200
Periodical volumes	15,000
Microfilm	3,000
Current periodical subscriptions	380
Date of completion	May 1984
Special equipment	Microfilm reader/printers, photocopy machines, terminals, IBM PC

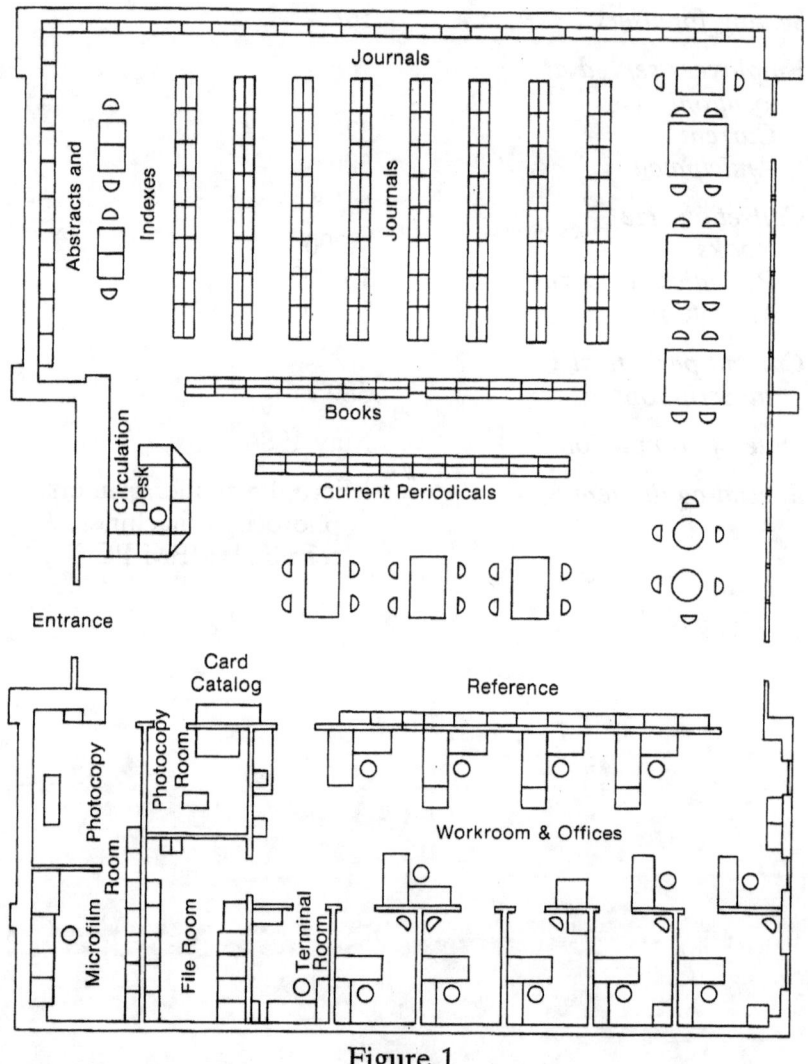

Figure 1

A New Pharmaceutical Company Library: The Upjohn Company Corporate Technical Library

Lorraine Schulte

ABSTRACT. In April of 1984, after 6 years of planning, the Upjohn Company Corporate Technical Library officially opened its new library facility in Kalamazoo, Michigan. A fairly large corporate library of some 25,000 square feet net usable space, it expressed a bold commitment to space for printed publications at a time when the paperless office and the paperless library were being widely touted. At the same time the new facility had to provide for the electronic library: over 70 electronic workstations, a User Search Lab, a Computer Room and an Online Training Center. The planning challenges, the rationale for space usage, and some of the special features of the new library are described.

The Upjohn Company is a worldwide, research-based producer and marketer of pharmaceuticals, health care services, fine chemicals, seed and agricultural specialties. Kalamazoo, Michigan serves as the corporate, research, and medical headquarters, and the home of its domestic pharmaceutical manufacturing organization. There are 22,000 Upjohn employees worldwide, approximately 8,000 in the Kalamazoo area, including 1200 research division personnel. Library information services are provided by the Corporate Technical Library, the Business Library and a Medical Information Unit that serves the medical division and the product information needs of

---

Lorraine Schulte is Associate Director, Technical Information Systems at the Upjohn Company, Kalamazoo, MI, and was formerly manager, Corporate Technical Library. She has a BS in Biology from New York State University College at Buffalo and the MSLS degree from Case Western Reserve University.

health care professionals. A number of unit (departmental) collections in Kalamazoo, and overseas subsidiary collections and information services, form an Upjohn library network. The Corporate Technical Library (CTL) has a staff of 39 including 18 library information professionals and 21 office staff. The mission of the Library is to provide systems, services, and expertise for selecting, managing, and disseminating technical information, both public and corporate, to Upjohn technical and management personnel, to support the growth and development of the pharmaceutical and agricultural businesses.

LIBRARY SERVICES

In addition to technical and information services common to most libraries, the Library has responsibility for several corporate information systems, and for research records management. Library staff create and maintain the corporate Product Information Retrieval System/Upjohn (PIRSU) database and a published product literature archive. PIRSU is searchable online from any Upjohn location worldwide. A parallel online information system for internal proprietary literature is also created and maintained by Library staff. The records management responsibility includes central filing of research records, filing policies and procedures, a uniform subject classification system, and electronic file training and consultation.

The Library is open 24 hours for company walk-in users, but is staffed only for the normal 8-hour day. A large portion of the client population, especially those offsite and overseas, access library services through telephone, teletype, and mail. Library information specialists and information scientists with degrees in both the chemical or biological sciences and library/information science, provide reference services, literature search services and current literature alerting. User education programs include an annual series of library seminars, tours and orientations for individuals or groups, instruction for specific subject area resources, and end-user online search training for the PIRSU product literature system and other commercially available bibliographic databases. Special current alerting publications are based on PIRSU and proprietary literature database updates.

All technical services operations—acquisitions, periodicals

control, bindery, cataloging—are supported by the LIS (Library Information System) integrated library automation system. The Corporate Technical Library provides periodical subscription and bindery services for clients as well as for the library collection, and it is the central cataloging unit for all Upjohn libraries and unit collections. A corporate online catalog is supported by LIS, as is automated circulation of library materials. Document delivery services are also provided.

LIBRARY COLLECTION

The size of the collection, especially the retention of bound periodicals (43,000 volumes), is a reflection of the geographic location of the library and the need to provide rapid turnaround on document requests. There are no nearby major medical, scientific or technical library resources for local document delivery backup. For a special library devoted primarily to current research, the Corporate Technical Library (CTL) must therefore keep a rather large number of older periodicals. Even though space for library materials is expensive, some of this cost is traded off against the ability to retrieve needed documents within 24 hours.

Special attention to collection control, not just development, is critical in this environment. The collection is reviewed annually for retention and discard decisions and there is an active program to convert medium use periodicals to 16 mm microfilm cartridges. These are interfiled alphabetically in the bound journal stacks. Product literature, technical reports, patents, and some periodical indexes are also kept on 16 mm microfilm cartridges. A weekly library publication announces additions to the CTL and the decentralized Unit Collections, new Upjohn authored publications and patents, and videotapes of in-house lectures and presentations from invited speakers.

LIBRARY SYSTEMS

Computer and computer-associated equipment in support of library systems and services is substantial, and during the planning process considerable attention was given to handling this equipment. There are over 70 electronic workstations in the library, not including Online Training Center equipment. If one were to count the number of associated devices such as printers, modems, graphic tablets, barcode readers, etc., the electronic equipment inventory numbers in excess of 180 items. Major systems components include 8 stations linked to a DEC WS248 processor for literature search downloading and editing; 16 terminals hardwired to the research division's mainframe for access to electronic mail, SAS-based library record keeping files, proprietary literature databases, and the STAIRS-based *Up*john *St*orgage *a*nd *R*etrieval *T*echnology (UPSTART) for personal bibliographic file management. The integrated library automation system, LIS (Library Information System) is run on a DEC PDP 11/44 and includes 26 stations in the Corporate Technical Library and 8 stations at decentralized Upjohn library and unit collection locations.

OLD FACILITY

The first Upjohn Technical Library was established in 1936 on the 7th floor of a combined manufacturing and research facility, at the interface between these 2 operations. An addition to this building in 1957 included a new and expanded library facility. Beginning in 1977, growth of staff and materials that could not be accommodated in the original facility began "budding" off into various locations at the downtown Kalamazoo research site. Although all of these were in buildings that could be reached on foot without going out-of-doors, by 1980 there was an unwieldy total of six CTL locations. Only the reference collection, the Information Services staff, the book collection, current periodicals, and a portion of the bound periodicals, remained in the original 7th floor library. Much user and staff space in the original library had been sacrificed to collection growth, and the rapidly developing electronic library was reaching the maximum capacity of the existing electric circuits in this old building.

PURPOSE OF THE NEW FACILITY

The new Corporate Technical Library facility was intended to provide adequate space for library clients, staff and collection growth for 10 years. A major focus of planning for the new facility, as already discussed, was the need to support a rapidly developing and changing electronic library. Functional departmental relationships that were lost when various library departments had moved to other research site locations, were to be reestablished. Improvements in access to the collection were expected through integration of all collections in one location. Control of the collection was also a major goal since decentralized and unstaffed collection locations, multiple exits that by-passed the circulation desk in the old library, and round-the-clock library hours were a problem.

PLANNING

Originally, expansion of the old library and remodeling of existing space at the research site were considered. The library's efforts to find space in existing facilities, pushing and squeezing at locations all over the downtown site, and other pressures on office and laboratory space, resulted in a complete space needs analysis and a long range space plan for the downtown site. The proposal finally approved was for a new seven-story multifunction research building, primarily for laboratories and animal rooms, with the second floor allocated for a new technical library. As with previous Upjohn research building projects, this multifunction research building was to be built as a shell with completion of a limited number of floors, including the library floor, in the original construction.

Planning began in earnest in early 1982. A library program of requirements, originally prepared in 1979, was revised and updated. The program statement contained information on the library's institutional environment, its mission, client population, collections, services, philosophy, space needs, and plans for the future. The program was a major tool for communicating the library's goals to the library design consultant, architects and other planners. Construction of the multifunction research building was to be carried out by an architectural and construction firm that had been involved in previous Upjohn research projects.

A library planning team was formed including the library manager, two additional library staff, representatives from

Upjohn Engineering, Pharmaceutical Research and Development Facilities Planning, Corporate Office Planning Services, and a contractor architect. Electrical, lighting and other specialty engineers, the library design consultant, and other library staff participated on the team as needed. The Library staff continued to work independently with the library design consultant who developed a number of schematics for alternative layouts. All library staff were involved in selection of the schematic of choice and from that scheme a detailed plan was produced by the library consultant. The schematics and early layout design was also shared with library clients to solicit input. The final plan was reviewed and approved by the Library Planning Team and construction drawings were produced by the building contractor.

DESIGN REQUIREMENTS AND BUILDING CONSTRAINTS

Although the library was to occupy the entire 30,000 gross square feet on the second floor of the new facility, a higher percentage (more than 15%) than would be expected in an office building of that size was not usable. Because construction had to accommodate laboratories and animal facilities, such things as multiple animal elevators in addition to passenger and freight elevators, took away much usable space.

The most significant contributor to loss of usable space was the utility shafts, two rows of which ran the entire 300 foot north/south length of the building. These shafts were very large, approximately $5' \times 10'$, to accommodate special laboratory chemical, air, and water handling needs. The shafts were no particular problem to a modular laboratory design, but presented a severe problem in creating a visually open and yet integrated library facility. The problem was solved quite effectively by incorporating these utility shafts into the office areas, and then building closets, photocopy and microfilm equipment into the alcoves created by the spaces between them, essentially hiding them.

This approach to hiding the shafts worked best if the majority of Library staff offices were to be located in the interior of the library. The north/south window walls could then be incorporated as part of the open area of the library where user seating and materials would be located. Although moving offices into the interior of the floor was a difficult decision for the staff to make, the superiority of this arrangement architecturally, functionally, and for the overall appearance of the library was clear to everyone.

THE NEW LIBRARY

Construction was begun in May of 1982 and the new Library opened in April of 1984. Moving was accomplished in a four-day period, including a weekend, with the assistance of a library moving firm and many staff. Moving offices and collections from six locations, and alphabetically integrating bound periodicals from 2 locations presented special challenges but there were no major moving problems.

Library materials capacity in the new facility is approximately 86,000 volumes. Although reference collection shelving is essentially filled to capacity, the collection is expected to remain stable at about 2,000 volumes. Reference collection expansion can be accommodated in the index and abstract area, if necessary. The area with relatively little growth space and the greatest capacity for growth is the bound journal area. To live in this space for even 10 years requires removal of about 300 linear feet of bound periodicals per year for each of the 10 years post-occupancy, either by discarding volumes or by microfilm conversion. To make reading and producing copies from the growing microfilm collection convenient, microfilm reader-printers are distributed throughout the bound journal stacks along with photocopy equipment.

Collections of scientific indexes, patents, product literature, and technical reports on 16 mm microfilm are housed centrally in a media area with reader-printers and other stations for slide/tape programs, videocassettes, etc. The Library's small collection of commercially available educational media is augmented by a large collection of videocassette recordings of weekly in-house lectures and presentations by visiting scientists. These are kept at the nearby circulation desk.

The reference (information) desk was placed near to the main center aisle, directly facing entering visitors. The desk was designed to hold 2-3 computer terminals and when necessary 2 staff. The computer equipment can be placed in any location on the desk and easily changed because of a wiring raceway built along the inside edge of the facing of the desk. The circulation desk was designed to accommodate a book card based circulation system for another year, and then LIS terminals for automated circulation. The circulation desk is just to the left as you enter the library. A Checkmate security system unit flanks the entry and serves as a reminder to appropriately charge library materials.

A display rack in a niche behind the reference desk holds regular library publications, the CTL News, Library Additions, Selected CTL Searches, Product Literature Alert, the Brief Guide to the CTL, and various request forms and "how to" handouts. It is specially mounted at a 45 degree angle so that the materials do not fall forward.

The carpet chosen for the Library includes both carpet tiles and broadloom. Taupe carpet tiles form the matrix in which islands of dark brown carpet tiles are placed to define seating areas and islands of deep royal blue broadloom define all stack areas. The sides and bases of all stacks are custom colored blue to match the broadloom on which they rest; remaining shelves are beige. All of the library furnishings in the public areas are finished in light oak with plum and blue upholstery accents.

Staff offices are by corporate policy open landscape plan offices. This design was followed in the new Corporate Technical Library with few exceptions. Attention was given to long term needs for equipment and the possibility of staff turnover, so that current technology and individual preference did not inhibit a good, flexible overall design. The modular office furniture with interchangeable, attached work surfaces and storage units, builds in a lot of that flexibility. Standard clerical office sizes had to be stretched somewhat to include in some cases as many as three different video display terminal workstations. In some processing areas, additional counters were planned near individual offices, and shared workstation areas (e.g., OCLC) were also developed. Fabric panels and chair upholstery for the open plan offices were by area, either oatmeal with plum accents or oatmeal with blue accents. Technical Services open plan offices were enclosed behind solid walls; Information Services open plan offices were left more accessible to the central public service area, the Reference Desk and the User Search Lab.

The Computer Room houses the DEC PDP 11/44 for the Library Information System; a DEC WS 248 system for on-line searching, downloading, and formatting; modems and the master cable patch panel; and various printers—a research mainframe printer, a high-speed printer on a leased line direct to a commercial database vendor, and a letter quality printer. The Computer Room required a raised floor to accommodate wiring associated with this equipment.

SPECIAL FEATURES

The current journal shelving was custom designed to allow for storage of multiple issues stacked cover outward on shelves which recline at a 5 degree angle. The issues are held in place by a clear plastic bookend, the base of which fits into a slot between the back and the bottom portion of the shelf. This type of shelving permits the journal covers themselves to serve as titles, eliminating the need to add, change and delete shelf label titles as the collection grows and changes. Individual shelf ends were also eliminated between each three-foot section of shelving, providing 12 linear feet of continuous self space per row. The current journal shelving can accommodate between 1,200 and 1,500 titles, depending on how closely the titles are packed in each 12 foot row.

Individual study carrels were designed so that the carrel wall on the window side was reduced to only a 2-inch height. This allowed for both a visually open appearance to the library and individual reader enjoyment. In addition to the twelve audio-visual stations centralized in the media area, four special purpose microfilm reader-printer carrels were designed for the bound journal stacks. A number of the individual study carrels were also wired to accommodate electronic equipment, including terminals for the online catalog in each of the three major stack areas (current journals, books, and bound journals).

File cabinet housing for a large collection of internal reports was used to create a partition for the circulation office area and placed back-to-back with a row of supply cabinets.

An H-shaped arrangement of light oak wooden end panels was made to surround the files and the supply cabinets, with a partition between them. The partition surface visible above the file cabinets (on back of the supply cabinets) was covered with the same fabric used on open landscape office partitions. The unit has created effective office privacy without obstructing the view past the circulation desk to the far end of the Library where monographs are shelved.

All new furniture was purchased and all old library furnishings replaced except for three card catalog units. Anticipating the arrival of an online catalog within a year of moving into the new Library, there was no reason to go to the expenditure of replacing the card catalog cabinets. Although we wanted to keep the card catalog units fairly close to the library entry and the central access points to the collection, their antique appearance was not at all compatible with the appearance of the new facility. Another custom designed H-shaped catalog unit, also in light oak, was the solution chosen for the card catalog problem. The unit was designed with counter space on one side for online catalog terminals and high stools; the other side had no counter, but framed the existing card catalog units. The unit was placed so that the card catalogs did not face the entry but the wall behind the reference desk instead. Three online catalog terminals are now in use on the front counter of this unit which also features an open raceway at the rear for easily moving equipment and wiring to different positions. In the coming year the card catalog will be removed from the back side of the unit and an additional counter can then be added.

Each of the Information Services area staff offices houses a computer terminal for literature searching and downloading. Two office spaces in this area house shared special use terminals (graphics and mainframe). A central collection of search stations was also made available in a User Search Lab: a research computer mainframe terminal; TTY terminal; a personal computer; and two chemical graphics stations, one DEC retrographics terminal, and an IBM PC/AT for both in-house and commercially available chemical graphics systems. Although a majority of the research staff have computer equipment in their offices and laboratories, developing end-user searchers, limited numbers of special purpose graphics terminals, and the convenience of accessing computer data files from the Library location, suggested the need for this kind of facility. The User Search Lab is also used for one-on-one end-user training and tutorials.

Approximately 2,000 square feet of library space were allocated to an Online Training Center with two classrooms. The larger room currently accommodates 12 mainframe and 12 PC stations, and the smaller room 5 office automation workstations. The facility is used for library end-user online search training, for research computer systems training, and corporate information systems training. The large classroom includes a video projector and an instructor video access network which permits viewing of individual workstation computer screens from the console at the front of the room. A mainframe printer and a laser printer for the Xerox office automation system are also located in a printer room in the facility.

Wire handling problems were a major concern in the Online Training Center and for a time it was thought that a raised floor might be required there too. Over a period of three to four years between initial planning and final construction, the design of the online workstation was constantly changing. The changes in information technology were moving rapidly and we seemed to be moving closer and closer to the universal electronic workstation. Although much special furniture had been developed to house individual electronic workstation set-ups, it was decided that a continuous counter would best help meet the objective of maximizing the class size for the facility and allowing maximum flexibility for equipment changes. Each 28 foot counter in the Online Training Center handles 6 workstations. All of the wiring comes up through the floor on one end of the room and is channeled into a continuous cabinet base under the workstations. This design helped avoid the expense of a raised floor. Access to the wiring channels is through small doors under each workstation. As in most other office areas of the Library where much video display terminal equipment is in use, a major consideration was given to lighting in the Online Training Center so that screen glare and reflection would be avoided. Pulling wiring from ceiling mounted cable trays on the first floor avoided the need for power poles anywhere in the library. Wiring was also well handled in the open plan offices where partitions are designed to carry and conceal wire in special channels.

In accordance with a company policy of supporting local and regional art, a variety of sculptures, tapestries, paintings, and limited edition prints were purchased for the Library.

OUTCOME

The overall results were extremely pleasing visually and a success functionally. The project was successful in meeting its primary objectives of adequate user and staff space, collection space, and electronic library facilities. The reaction from clients and upper management has been overwhelmingly positive.

Problems with the new facility were limited. A significant staff adjustment to open plan offices was required, especially because white noise originally planned for the library floor had been eliminated as an economy measure. Each staff member has an individual office with visual and psychological privacy, but normal office conversation and telephone calls can be overheard many offices away. Careful attention to modulating conversation volume and just plain learning to live with it has helped. A new telephone system currently being implemented will permit variable ring tone and ring patterning that should help distinguish multidepartmental calls within large office spaces.

There was some concern with lighting in the public reception areas and over the study carrels. Metal halide downlights created a very dramatic effect in these areas, but their localized intensity created glare interrupted by dark spots and shadows over the circulation and reference desks. The downlights in these areas were exchanged for fluorescent lighting with parabolic lenses. All offices have finished ceilings with flourescent lights and parabolic lenses. Unfinished, exposed ceilings in the bound journal and book stack areas were painted black and equipped with fluorescent lighting (with light modulating Fresnel lenses) running perpendicular to the shelving at stack top height. The lighting defines the effective ceiling height in these stack areas.

The microfilm carrels custom designed for the large microfilm reader-printers proved somewhat bulky and needed modification for convenient operation of the equipment. Modifications to the online catalog unit were also made to improve wire handling, essentially hiding the traverse of wires from the counter to the floor. "New book shelf" units made of oak were recently wall mounted in a prominent location in the reference area. The 2,000 volume shelving limit for the reference collection did not allow sharing even 12 linear feet of that space for new book display.

Other recent additions have been a computer room security system requiring authorized I.D. badge access after hours. A special alarm system monitoring temperature and humidity was also installed. The room has its own self-contained air cooling system.

Closets for storage and coats were designed into the utility shaft alcoves and at other locations, but storage space is still tight. It seems it is almost impossible to plan too much storage or unplanned space; we wish we had a bit more. There was a sharp limit on the space we could plan for staff expansion within the allocated space; addition of more than two new staff will surely send us to the shelf areas for space to convert to additional offices. This might also help push the adoption of alternative storage media, such as optical disc, and/or access to electronic journals.

Two years of occupancy have not uncovered any major problems or concerns about what might have been. The Library appears to be wearing rather well, already accommodating equipment, office and staffing changes. Continued attention to consistency in choice of colors and design for library furnishings, accessories, signage, etc., will aid in keeping the facility looking new for many years to come.

STATISTICS

Gross area	30,000 sq. ft.
Net usable space	25,000 sq. ft.
Date of completion	April 1984
Staff	
Professional	18
Nonprofessional	21

Employees served at
  location   8000

Seating
  Carrels   27
  Index/abstract stations   18
  Av/microfilm stations   20
  Table seats   40
  Lounge chairs   18

Collection Size	Collection	Capacity
Books	15,000	24,000
Reference collection	2,000	2,000
Indexes/abstracts	3,200	6,600
Bound journal volumes	43,000	53,000
Current monographic serials	400	" "
Current periodical subscriptions	1,200	1,500

Services
  Circulation   20,000
  Document delivery requests   54,000
  Current alerting profiles   1,000
  Literature search requests   3,600

Equipment
  LIS integrated library system
    terminals   26
  Research computer mainframe
    terminals   16
  OCLC stations   3
  FAXON datalinx terminals   4
  Downloading and data capture
    stations   8
  Chemical structure search
    stations   3
  Xerox word processing
    stations   5
  General purpose search
    terminals   8

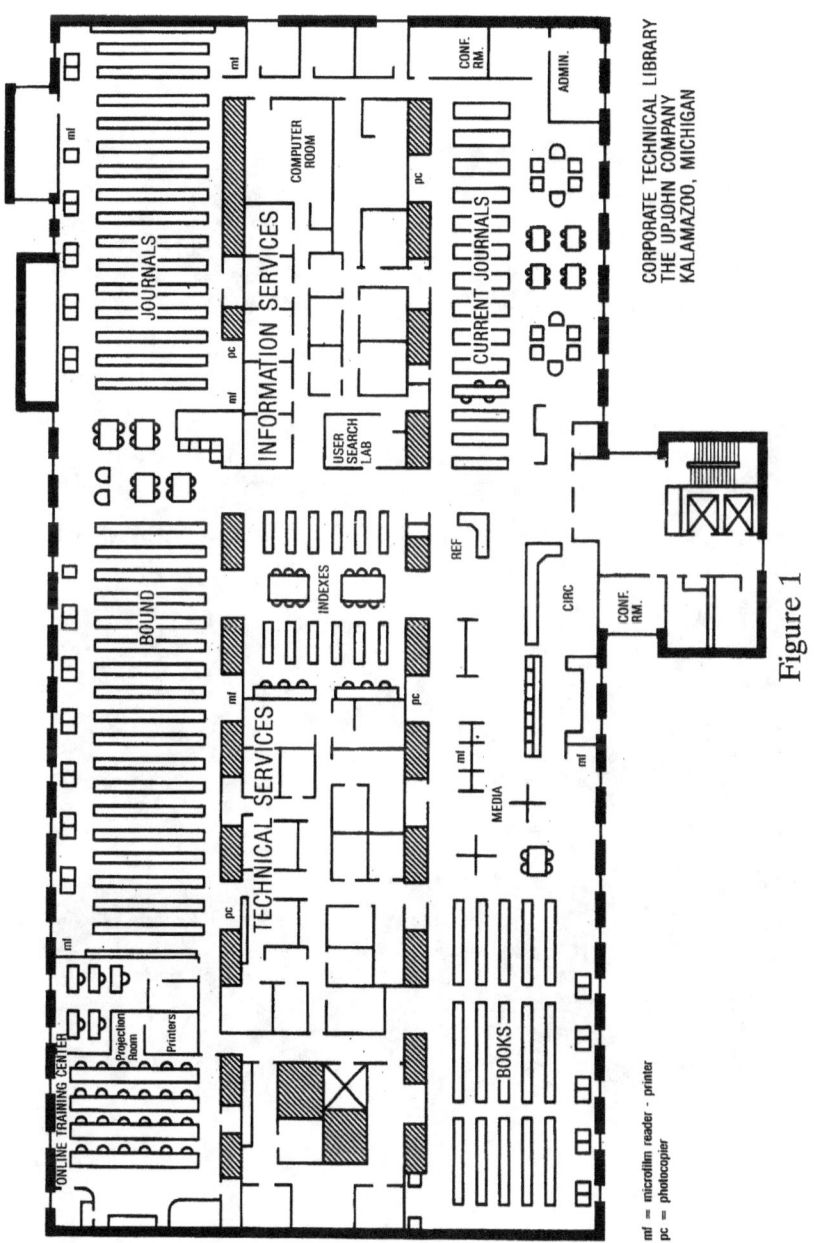

Figure 1

Figure 2

The John Crerar Library of the University of Chicago

Patricia K. Swanson

ABSTRACT. The merger of the John Crerar Library with the University of Chicago is summarized. The new facility built to house the combined collections is described. The mission and services of the new library are noted.

The design of the new John Crerar Library reflects the nature of the clientele it serves, the collections it houses, the services offered and the history and traditions of the two institutions which merged to create the new library. Opened in September 1984, the building is the culmination of years of planning.

HISTORY AND BACKGROUND

The Crerar Library was established in 1984 by a bequest from Chicago railroad industrialist, John Crerar (1827–1889). Since it opened its doors in 1897, the Crerar has been a significant repository for scientific, medical and technical materials. The Library's first Board of Directors specified the subjects of the collection to complement the recently founded Newberry Library and the Chicago Public Library. Crerar's original scope also included philosophy, applied fine arts, sociology and economics.[1] In the 1950's Crerar sold most of these collections to concentrate on science, medicine and

---

Patricia K. Swanson holds a BS in English and Education from the University of Missouri and an MLS from Simmons College. Her present position is Assistant Director for Science Libraries at the University of Chicago, The John Crerar Library, 5730 South Ellis Avenue, Chicago, IL 60637. James Vaughn and Kathleen Zar of the Crerar Library provided substantial assistance in the writing of this article.

© 1986 by The Haworth Press, Inc. All rights reserved.

technology. Several research libraries in the United States now hold collections which were once part of the Crerar.

Originally housed in rental space in the Marshall Field Building in Chicago's Loop, the Crerar Board purchased property and built quarters at the corner of Randolph Street and Michigan Avenue. Crerar provided service from this location from 1921 until 1962. Although centrally located, these facilities became seriously overcrowded and lacked the flexible space required for rapidly growing collections. In 1962 a contractual agreement was established between the Illinois Institute of Technology (IIT) and Crerar in which the library would move to a new building on the IIT campus and would provide resources and services to IIT faculty and students. In 1980, in terms satisfactory to both parties, Crerar and IIT decided to terminate the contractual relationship by 1984. In 1981, the Crerar Board of Directors and the University of Chicago Board of Trustees signed a legal document of merger that would bring the Crerar Library permanently to the University.

Although several years in the discussion stage, planning for the library officially began in April 1981 when a formal, legal agreement between the Crerar Board of Directors and the University of Chicago Board of Trustees was signed. Under the terms of this agreement, the assets of Crerar (endowment and collections) were transferred to the University of Chicago and a new library to house the collections was built. The University assumed financial and operating responsibility, agreed to retain the name, the John Crerar Library, in perpetuity, and committed itself to the tenets of Crerar's Last Will and Testament which specified that the Library be open to the public. The officers of both organizations worked together to raise funds for the building. The Crerar Library, housed at the Illinois Institute of Technology under contractual arrangements with that institution, also made formal agreements with officials at IIT for the staged withdrawal of collections. Under the agreements, all activities were to be completed before December, 1984. A merger of this size and complexity is unprecedented in American research library history.

The John Crerar Library and the University of Chicago, both founded in the last decade of the 19th century, have always been conscious of each other in collecting policies, scope and emphasis. Thus at the time of the merger, there was less than forty percent duplication. Crerar's holdings in medicine, applied science and technology complemented the University's basic and theoretical holdings. Intellectually, the two libraries fit together elegantly.

Bibliographically, they were less compatible. Crerar used Dewey classification; the University, Library of Congress. Crerar cataloged on OCLC, the University on its own Library Data Management System (LDMS). Now only Library of Congress classification is being used for new materials added for all conversion of Crerar unique titles. Cataloging is being done on LDMS and added to OCLC through the University's tape-loading membership.

The University Director, Martin Runkle, working with the Trustees, University administrators and the University architects, created the building program statement, reviewed requirements, selected the architects and chose the site. Soon after the basic outlines of the building had been determined, the Directors of both libraries decentralized the planning process. Not only were there faculty and Crerar corporate users committees, there were also task forces of librarians who defined space requirements and appropriate service relationships, specified the stack arrangements and defined the collections to be located in the new library.[2,3]

THE MOVE

The move into the new building was preceded by an inventory of the two collections to identify duplicates which could be sold. The collections consisted of 770,000 volumes from Crerar and 400,000 science volumes from Chicago. These were housed in seven different locations and shelved in over a dozen call number sequences. Duplicates to be sold were sorted out. Unique volumes from both collections and over 37,000 duplicates used to fill gaps or as added copies were retained. Most were integrated into one call number sequence during the move. The integration of the Dewey sequences was completed during the summer of 1985.

Prior to the move, Library staff decided to select over 3,000 biomedical serial titles to be arranged alphabetically rather than by call number in the new building. Once the titles were selected by the bibliographer, the work began locating these titles, measuring the space required and planning for their rearrangement during the move. Changing the arrangement of over 100,000 volumes from call number to alphabetical title order was an added complication, but has paid off in favorable patron reaction and in ease of access.

The fundamental principle underlying the move was to minimize service interruptions and all strategies for the move conformed to that principle. Least-used material was moved first. Some Crerar material was moved to campus storage as early as 1982 and later moved into the new building. The Chicago medical collections and all current periodicals were moved from their public locations last—some just hours before the new building's opening on September 10, 1984. Crerar on the IIT campus closed on July 31, 1984. Telephone access for reference and photocopy service was available throughout August. There was no direct access to the Crerar collections during August; however, all materials could be paged by users from the University's Regenstein Library. Although this focus on availability heightened the complexity of the move, its public relations value was inestimable.

THE MISSION OF THE NEW LIBRARY

The mission of the new John Crerar Library is to serve the instructional and research needs of the University of Chicago faculty, staff and students, (including the Medical Center), to support the longstanding Corporate Members' Program, to serve as Resource Library in the Regional Medical Library Network, to serve as a Special Resource Library in ILLINET and to serve the scientific public. Services are focused on acquiring, processing and interpreting strong collections, aiding in the discovery of literature through traditional reference service and computer literature searching, procuring materials not locally owned when needed by users, providing quarters for quiet study and research, and making the facility and the collections open to eligible users round-the-clock.

Technology used to support these functions includes Public Access Terminals to the University's Library Data Management System (LDMS) for all materials added since 1974, all active serials and all conversion project titles, circulations and reserve automated systems, as well as computer access to external databases, electronic mail and telefacsimile transmission. Over 90,381 science monographic titles and 21,093 science serial titles are in LDMS as of November 1985. More are being added each day, either through current purchasing or through retrospective conversion projects. The value of LDMS to the merger effort was substantial. Its capabilities permitted large scale record changes to reflect changed locations of material, permitted quick additions to the file of converted monographs or Crerar unique serial titles and gave a bibliographic unity to a dramatically changed library situation.

SERVICE CONCEPTS UNDERLYING THE DESIGN OF THE NEW LIBRARY

The broad service mission; the varied, yet sophisticated research clientele for this library; the requirement for round-the-clock access; the need for economy in staffing, operations and maintenance; the anticipation of continued growth of both printed and microform collections; and present and potential impacts of technology all heightened the requirements for flexibility and influenced the design of this library.

These factors resulted in a simple building, with one public entrance, services and staff concentrated on the main floor, open stacks, a single call number sequence and reader tables and carrels around the periphery of each stack floor and on the main floor directly adjacent to library material. The building's simplicity and flexibility were easier to execute because many library functions, such as technical services, preservation, personnel and administrative support and special collections (rare books and archives) are provided through the University Library's main unit, Regenstein Library.

New services and policies introduced at the time the facility opened were welcomed by users and enhanced the library in their eyes. A major service improvement was the introduction of Public Access Terminals. Learning to query the terminals for bibliographic information was just one more new feature and users learned it along with learning their way around the library. The non-circulation of bound and unbound serials was a policy requested by faculty and supported by library staff. Introducing it required careful planning, publicity and firmness. This policy, coupled with the vast amount of material, formerly spread throughout several departmental libraries and in storage, now housed in one location, dramatically increased the ease of access to material for scientists. Such a change in policy to non-circulation, often so hard to introduce, has been widely supported in this new facility. A library-wide no smoking policy was in place from the first day of service. This policy has been easily accepted. Smoking is permitted in the canteen on the Lower Level, outside the Library control area. The opening of a new library is an opportune time to start new services and policies that might be more difficult to introduce as changes in an established facility.

DESCRIPTION OF THE FACILITY

The design of the new John Crerar Library aimed at not only creating a distinctive building for the campus, but also carrying on the planning and heritage begun by the architects who designed the original buildings on campus. The new library's limestone facade, form, mass, scale, window treatment and detail, such as a freestanding arch at the main entrance reinforce the gothic traditions of the campus. The limestone cantilevers on the exterior of the third floor shade the building, thus shielding the interior from ultraviolet light and adding protection from heat.

Located on the west side of a new science quadrangle, the library is in close proximity to the laboratories, offices and classrooms of the scientists and students it serves. One special feature is an underground passageway connecting the library to the Cummings Life Sciences Center and to the University Medical Center.

The building is rectangular, has four floors—three above ground and one below grade. It has 160,000 gross square feet and 143,000 assignable square feet. The approximate east-west dimension is 135 feet and the north-south dimension is 294 feet. The Library has capacity for 1.3 million volumes. There are presently just over 900,000 volumes in the building.

The main floor features the primary entrance, circulation, reserves, reference, computer search services, librarians' offices, current periodicals, a new materials display area, photocopy machine rooms, a microforms room, administrative offices, technical processing (periodical check-in claiming and bindery preparation) and the loading dock. There are study tables for 182 readers.

The Second Floor contains stacks for the clinical medicine and biological sciences (QH-QR, R), four group study rooms, four small faculty study rooms, two photocopy machine rooms, typing rooms, directory kiosks, telephones for library assistance and for medical staff to respond to telepages, and tables and carrels for 212 readers.

The Third Floor contains stacks for the general sciences, physical sciences, agriculture, engineering and technology collections (GC, Q, QB, QC, QE, S and T). QA and QD are in separate math and chemistry libraries located elsewhere on campus. Other facilities are the same as on the second floor. There are tables and carrels for 220 readers.

The Lower Level contains the unique Dewey collections in all subjects not yet converted to LC classification. These collections are shelved on Spacesaver compact shelving. Study spaces for 36 readers are adjacent to the compact shelving. The Photocopy and Interlibrary Lending Department, the National Translations Center, a computer terminal cluster (operated by the University's Computation Center), a conference room with a kitchen, and a staff lounge are on the west side of the lower level. A public canteen and coin-operated lockers are on the east side of the Lower Level, accessible only from the front entrance of the Library and outside the Library's entrance control area.

Throughout the building, recessed fluorescent lighting is arranged perpendicular to the stacks to insure good lighting even if the stacks are rearranged. The interior furnishings are warm colors and accented with natural light oak.

A highlight of the new library is the three-story atrium at the south end of the new building which provides natural light, a sense of space and an orientation to the entire building. In the atrium hangs "Crystara," a large sculpture constructed of aluminum and Waterford crystal by John David Mooney.

The architecture of the new library received attention in

journals and in the press. One writer noted that the University of Chicago's "conceptually comprehensive campus plan" has been extended successfully in the new John Crerar Library.[4-6] Another that the the new building "will carry its vines gracefully."[7]

PROBLEMS IN THE NEW LIBRARY

The problems discovered in the first year are miniscule when compared to the successes of this straightforward, functional, lovely building. Describing them focuses our attention to correct them and may alert other librarians designing buildings to avoid them.

The intrusion and fire security systems are complex, yet not always effective. More attention should have been paid to who would be onsite after regular library hours and who should be authorized to reset the system. The panels are over-elaborate and the light signals seem contrary to common sense.

Minor adjustments to the heating, cooling and ventilation systems are still needed. The north end of the building was extremely cold last winter, while the south end was too warm. Humidity has been too high in some areas.

Eight small faculty study rooms were added late in the planning, after original plans had called for more. These rooms are too small, too close to each other to permit typing without disturbing neighbors and are poorly ventilated. In retrospect there should either have been more and larger studies or none.

All the study tables have low dividers to encourage higher utilization of space. This has inconvenienced readers who wish to spread out folios or other large volumes. A mix of divided and undivided tables would have given readers more options.

THE FUTURE OF A CENTRALIZED SCIENCE LIBRARY

The new John Crerar Library is a bold statement by the University that most of its internationally known faculty can be well-served by a large central science library with only 2 additional small campus facilities. The basic and theoretical orientation of many of the University's research programs, a long tradition of interdisciplinary research and an emphasis on the search for new knowledge, all speak to the need for a central library with broad and deep research collections. The compact size of the campus and its growth through careful planning have put most scientists' offices, laboratories and classrooms in reasonable proximity to the spot where the library now stands.

There will always be practical and political tensions between the advantages of large centralized collections and the advantages of smaller collections next door to the laboratory. These tensions will be addressed in different ways at different institutions. The University of Chicago's model of predominantly centralized science collections and services with planned divergence for special needs or geographic distance is a sound one for the present and the foreseeable future.

The present is exciting at the new John Crerar Library and prospects for the immediate future seem bright. The faculty, students and staff of the Biological Sciences Division, the University Medical Center, and the Physical Sciences Division are better served than in the past in terms of facilities, hours of service, hours of access, amount of material available on open shelves and concentrations of staffing to provide both general and specialized assistance. The Corporate members are using the library effectively and the public has access to the library under the terms of John Crerar's will. Sustaining the momentum of this success, moving into the future with new technology and possibly collections in new formats will be our challenge in the years to come.

STATISTICS

Architects	The Stubbins Associates Cambridge, Massachusetts
Associate architects	Loebl, Schlossman and Hackl Chicago, Illinois

Movers	Hallett and Sons Chicago, Illinois
Size	160,836 gross sq. ft. 143,000 assignable
Seating for users	680
Volume capacity	1.3 Million 770,000 volumes/conventional shelving 530,000 volumes/compact shelving
Cost	$22 million—including all fees, construction furnishings, equipment, landscaping, site preparation, moving, merger and other costs
Date of completion	September 1984
Average number of users per week	7,000
Collection size	920,000 volumes
Current periodical subscriptions	6,000

Staff Size
  Professional
  Non-professional
	
	9
	30

REFERENCES

1. Bay, J. Christian. *The John Crerar Library, 1895–1944: an historical report prepared under the authority of the Board of Directors.* Chicago: 1945: Chaps. 1, 3, 10.

2 Swanson, Patricia. Planning as job enrichment: a case study. *Journal of Academic Librarianship.* 9(6): 350–351; 1984 January.

3. Cairns, Paul. Chicago/Crerar Merger. *Library Resources and Technical Services.* 30 (2): 1986 April–June. (In press.)

4. A question of context. *Architectural Record.* 173 (8): 94–97; 1985 August.

5. Holton, Felicia Antonelli. For scientists, business and the public—a striking new science library. *University of Chicago Magazine.* 77(2): 12–15, 51; 1985 Winter.

6. Gapp, Paul. New Crerar Library: a building that succeeds in function and esthetics. *Chicago Tribune.* (Section 13):14; 1985 Sunday, May 19.

7. Davidson-Powers, Cynthia. The John Crerar Library. *Inland Architect.* 29(3): 30–32; 1985 May/June.

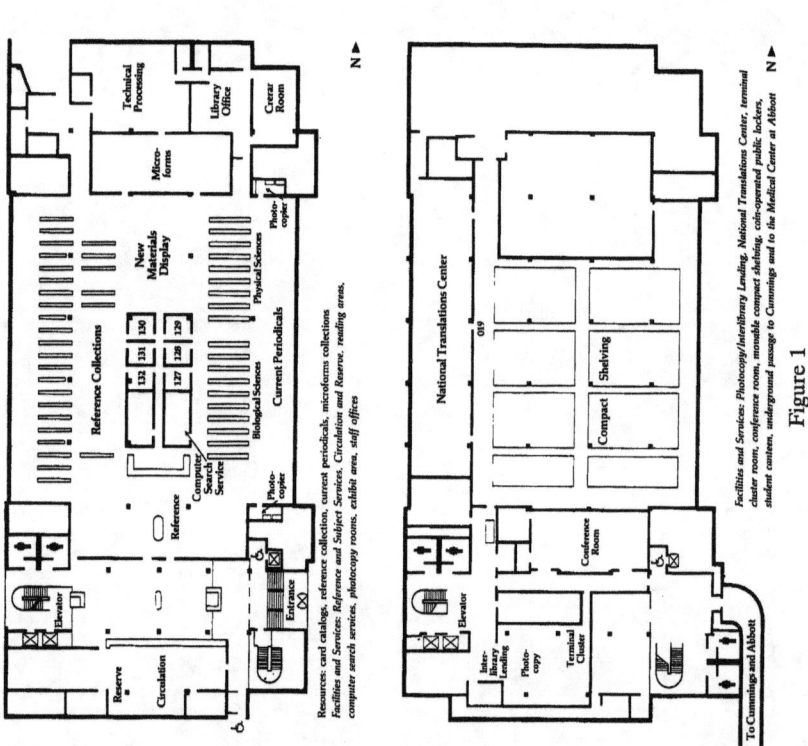

Figure 1

Figure 2
Photo by Jim Wright.

The New O'Callahan Science Library at the College of the Holy Cross

Tony Stankus

ABSTRACT. Features of a new facility at the named institution are discussed. Special mention is made of a unique reference station, a mobile compact shelving unit, and a split-level librarian's suite that features a loft office and a ground-level bibliographic instruction space. The role of the library's permanent displays in shaping student awareness of research for publication is emphasized.

MOTIVATION

The impetus for a new Science Library at the College of the Holy Cross was sustained by physical need, institutional traditions, and competitive recruitment factors. The original Science Library was founded in 1958. It was a consolidation of separate Biology, Chemistry, Mathematics, and Physics libraries plus the general science collection in the main library of the campus. It totalled approximately 12,000 volumes. The original capacity was 48 seats and 25,000 volumes. Seating was equally divided between small 2-ft. × 3-ft. carrels and crowded 3-ft. × 8-ft. six-person tables. Each of the three balconies held 8,000 volumes, with 1,000 volumes of ground-floor shelving. By the early 1970's it was apparent that with an annual growth rate of approximately 800 monographs and 1,200 bound periodicals, more space would be quickly needed. An earnest program of weeding subtracted a remark-

---

Tony Stankus is Science Librarian at College of the Holy Cross, Worcester, MA 01610. He took his BA *Summa Cum Laude* from Holy Cross, and his MLS from the University of Rhode Island. He has been the Science Librarian at Holy Cross since 1974.

© 1986 by The Haworth Press, Inc. All rights reserved.

able 6,000 monographs. Older bound periodicals totalling 14,000 volumes were gradually shipped over to the main library. Space for 4,000 volumes was created by trade-offs in seating. Nonetheless, by 1980 it was apparent that some fundamental solution must be carried out.

Yet it was quickly decided that one option—closing the Science Library and remerging it into the newly-expanded main library—would not be done. The rejection of this plan had nothing to do with any deficiency of the main library's excellent staffing or management. Rather, the most suasive arguments stemmed from the school's distinctive tradition and enduring prospects in the sciences. The school numbers among its alumni members of the National Academy of Sciences, tenants of endowed scientific chairs, deans of medical schools, an editor with the *New England Journal of Medicine,* and a director of a member institute of the National Institutes of Health. Despite its comparatively tiny 2,400 strictly undergraduate enrollment, the school is one of the top 20 national producers of American Chemical Society-accredited bachelor degree chemists, and is a top-100 source of medical school graduates. Future interest in the sciences also appears strong. The school currently receives about 4,800 applicants for its 600 freshman seats, with about twenty percent indicating an interest in science majors or premedical preparation.

Added to the internal forces were competitive factors. While many liberal arts colleges (particular small Catholic ones) are not noted for substantial laboratory facilities or sustained funding for the sciences, distinguished exceptions tend to maintain sizeable, independent science libraries. While havings its own character and mission, Holy Cross competes to some degree with these secular schools for students and faculty, and has always sought to maintain a certain comparability of quality. Indeed, by the time a decision to move on with the new Library was made, a whole new building incorporating a number of science department improvements was involved. In its library aspects the plan benefitted from data or layouts from a number of model institutions: Carleton, Colgate, Earlham, Haverford, Hope, Smith, St. Olaf, Swarthmore, Wellesley, and Wesleyan.

ASSEMBLING THE TEAM

The first step towards a new library was a consultant's report from Jay Lucker, Director of MIT's libraries. Its essence was that a new facility should have 10,000 sq. ft., in which 100 students and 100,000 volumes might be housed. When these recommendations were accepted and became a mandate from the Board of Trustees, the second step, the gathering together of a working design group began.

Both on-campus and off-campus expertise would be needed. The local group consisted of the Science Librarian, the Head Librarian and his Assistant. The Director of Physical Plant and Purchasing made a number of suggestions. Input from faculty, students, and other library staff was encouraged and is now acknowledged.

The outside expertise and leadership was of course chiefly supplied by the architects, Otis Robinson, Principal, and Robert Tacconi, Associate, of the Boston firm Shepley, Bullfinch, Richardson and Abbott. Nonetheless, representatives from the contractor, Perini Corporation, played a major role in several decisions. The entire process was one of frequent and very frank exchanges of proposals and counterproposals. Factors of money and construction timetables weighed heavily. Perhaps most symbolic was the fact that the Science Librarian used up three one-hundred foot rolls of architect's tracing paper in eighteen months—with each roll freely given by these most understanding architects!

IDENTIFYING MAJOR GOALS

Increases in quantity were the most obvious goals: more space, more shelving, more seating, etc. Yet variety and quality were equal considerations: specialty shelving in special circumstances and a return to at least two types of seating. The new library would have tailored shelving for the reference collection, new book selection, and current periodicals that differed substantially from that used for the regular monographs and bound periodicals. It was decided that a simple build-up of seating back to 1958 levels of carrels and open tables would be unsatisfactory. As further discussions showed, lounge seating, enclosed seminar rooms, specialized counters and the like were added as appropriate. Equipment and space for computers, videos, and microforms would, for the first time, be included in the plan. Even considerations of access to the library and traffic patterns within it were judged capable of improvement. Indeed, there was no sentiment for a repeat of the multifloor design of the old library. A ground-floor location with ease of entry for the handicapped, and at a confluence of stairways and elevators for the mobile, was deemed desirable.

THE RESULTS—LEFT WING

The new Science Library was in fact ultimately located on the ground floor of the new Swords Hall. This new structure is located between the two existing science buildings and connects to them by glass-enclosed malls. The Science Library's main entrance is adjacent to the larger of the malls. Owing to the Library's own glass walls, library customers have visual access not only to a landscaped terrace at the mall's entrance, but the mall's tree-lined walkways and benches. Customers may reach the library from any one of the complex's labs or classes without ever going outdoors. Indeed, patrons have a choice of four stairway routes or a 10-ft. × 12-ft. elevator when going to the library.

The first views of an entering patron include four common library features and an uncommon number of glass-enclosed display cases. Directly ahead is the photocopy machine and a display case. Directly to the right is the circulation/reserve desk, with the reference station twelve feet in front. These two areas are divided by another display case. Finally, farther to the right, and adjacent to the circulation/reserve desk is the card catalog and on-line catalog area. Once again, the area is flanked by a number of wall-display cases. While the photocopier, circulation/reserve, and catalog areas are certainly attractive, they are rather typical in layout and size. The more unique feature are the emphasis on display and the handling of the reference station.

The function of the display cases is one of reminder and

reenforcement. They seek to teach the student the role of journal publications in the progress of science and individual careers. One set of cases contains our own faculty's recent papers. Another contains the papers of prominent alumni. That our efforts at instruction have borne some fruit is apparent in the third set of cases, for these contain student papers accepted in refereed journals.

The reference area is a story of engineering necessity turning into architectural virtue. Designers were confronted with two 12-ft. × 12-ft. utility shafts placed in rather prominently visible areas of the library, one to each wing. The solution was to wrap a 2-ft. wide counter and specially-tailored reference book shelving all the way around each shaft. Each now has 48 linear feet of attractive consulting and seating space, and ample capacity for the intended collections.

Library customers who proceed further into the wing have a choice of either the current periodicals/new books area or the regular monograph stacks. The new books/periodicals area is arguably the most prominent spot in the library. It is surrounded by glass giving mall pedestrians a striking view of our 30-foot long current journal display case. One side of the case is served by three 4-ft. × 6-ft. four-person tables. The other is served by six semi-lounge chairs with adjoining coffee tables. The choice location and special accommodations given to current periodicals is in line with not only their importance to science in general, but serves as yet another reminder to students of where we expect them to make their mark.

Yet the monographs area is scarcely substandard. The area is served by expansive 2-ft. × 4-ft. custom-built carrels. Along each is a conduit for computer cabling should we wish to convert some work stations.

The central portion of the library layout is dominated by a series of rooms. There are two 9-ft. × 12-ft. group studies. Each has a 4-ft. × 6-ft. table, 4 chairs, a bookcase and a chalkboard. These are principally used for problem sessions and group projects. There are three other 12-ft. × 16-ft. special function rooms, each having a 2-1/2 ft.-wide counter along two walls, with seating for six. These rooms are slated to gradually become, respectively, a microform room, a videotape room, and a computer room. Each room is computer cabled and extensively wired. Equipment will be purchased and installed incrementally. One of our surprises is that even now students seem to prefer these wide counter study spaces.

Yet another room in the area is the split-level librarian's suite. The librarian's personal working space is a 9-ft. × 12-ft. loft with a panoramic view overlooking the left wing. The remaining space has a 12-ft. × 16-ft. area. It features a 12-ft. conference table, seating for ten, a chalkboard and a projection screen. Its function includes bibliographic instruction and staff meetings.

Finally, there is a 12-ft. × 12-ft. combination work room and assistant's office, with not only the usual typing station and desk but ample cabinetry and counter space for processing reserve books and bindery.

THE RESULTS—RIGHT WING

The right wing contains many of the same features found in the left wing. The wrap-around reference station with seating of the left wing is here the center of an indexing-abstracting quadrant. It serves to house *Science Citation Index*. The number, size and type of carrels in the rest of the wing are much the same. There is however much more conventional shelving than in the monographic wing with all of the remaining space devoted to alphabetically-arranged bound periodicals. There is an 80-ft. long counter running along the wall with no seating, to facilitate consulting.

Clearly, the most striking feature of the wing is the mobile, compact storage shelving. The installation consists of two separate units, each having ten 12-ft., double-faced bookcases. Each movable bookcase has a crank and literally glides along a track with a turn involving only four pounds of pressure. These units, manufactured by Acme Visible File Company, and marketed as "Magic Aisle 820", have proven easy to operate, safe, and entirely accurate in their space-saving claims. The only drawback has been the need to have re-levelling performed from time to time. These units are used for runs of dead or older bound periodicals. A final feature of the wing is a remarkable 6-ft. × 70-ft. storage tunnel currently used for supplies and shelving, as well as unprocessed donations.

CUSTOMER RELATIONS

The response to the new facility can honestly be reported as overwhelmingly favorable. Typical daily attendance has tripled. Circulation of new books, now featured in their own display area, is almost 100 percent of arrivals. Interestingly, faculty who have always had current journal sign-out privileges have tended to do more of their reading within the library and less in their offices. There is now less of a problem of loose-issue retrieval at bindery time. One major surprise is the consistent preference of many student users for the counter-type seating available in a number of locations within the library. The display areas receive substantial notice from students and faculty, both of whom are now quick to bring their reprints to the librarian. The entire facility is on the tour of every organized group of prospective students, alumni, donors, or granting agencies. Every faculty candidate is given an extended personal tour by the Science Librarian.

Outside groups have been favorably impressed, including a number of regional and state library associations. We have successfully hosted a number of regional disciplinary conferences, principally in chemistry, and a national meeting of the American Mathematical Society.

OPTIONS FOR THE FUTURE

As new as the library is, it too will one day be crowded. We have reinforced a floorspace in the existing left wing for installation of yet another 22,000-volume rolling compact storage unit, and stand ready to add up to 45 computer terminals on the enlarged carrels as necessary. We can add up to thirty more seats by reducing the somewhat generous floorspace allotments we currently use back down to standard.

SUMMARY OF FEATURES

Before	*After*
2,400 sq. ft.	10,500 sq. ft.

24 (2 ft. × 3 ft.) carrels	45 (2 ft. × 4 ft.) carrels
4 (3 ft. × 8 ft.) tables for 6	5 (4 ft. × 6 ft.) tables for 4 6 semi-lounge seats with coffee tables
25,000 vol. designed capacity	93,000 vol. designed capacity with 22,000 volumes of existing rolling compact shelving, additional unit possible for future expansion
6 cases, current periodicals	20 cases, current periodicals
1 case, new books	4 cases, new books Numerous display cases Special space for bibliographic instruction (10 additional seats) Special rooms for computers, videos and microforms (18 additional seats) Special stations for reference and abstracts (32 additional seats) Special storage and work rooms

---

Existing Collection (approx.)

19,000 monographs
25,000 bd. periodicals
400 current subscriptions

Primary Clientele

51 sci. faculty & technicians
400 sci. majors & premeds

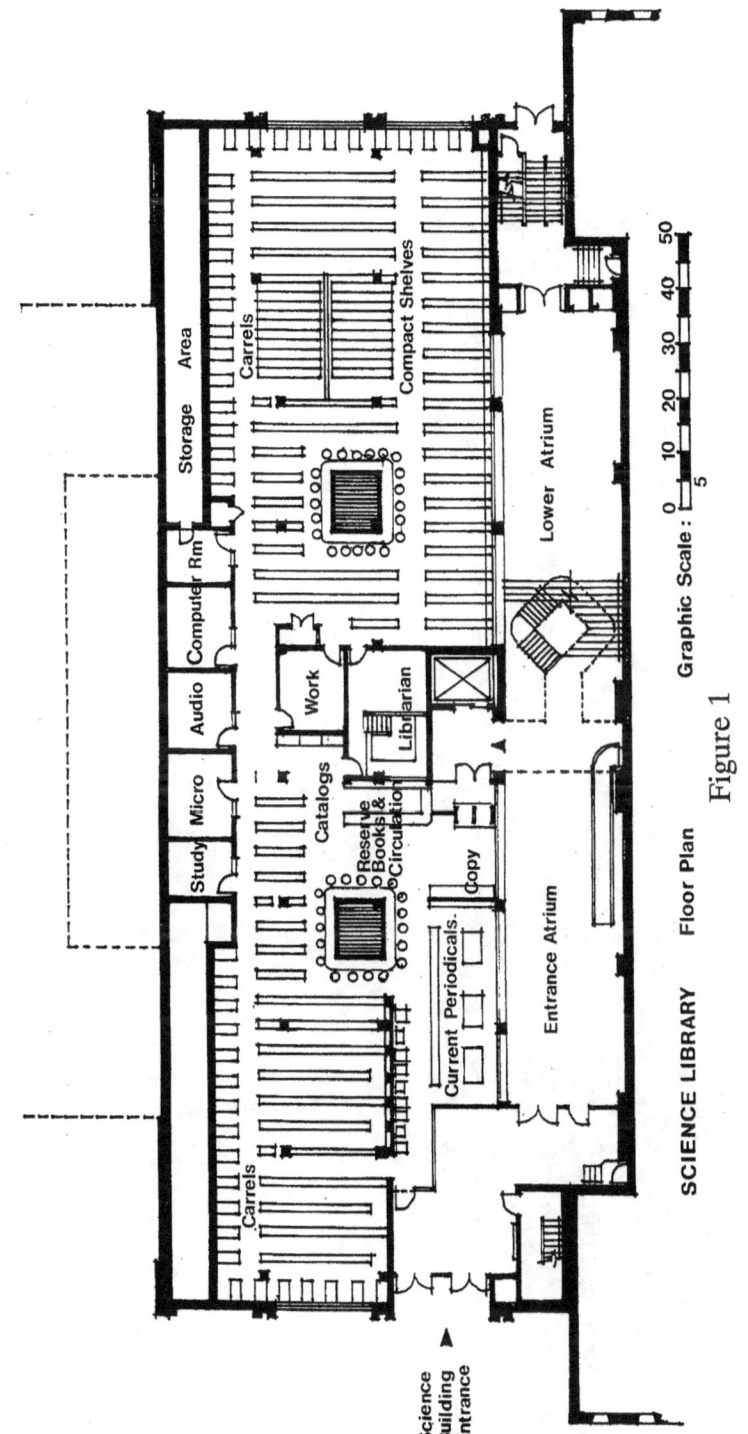

SCIENCE LIBRARY   Floor Plan

Figure 1

One of the more unusual features of Holy Cross College's new Science Library is a successful installation of mobile compact storage shelving. (Acme Magic Aisle 820—A Michael J. Novia photo.)

One side of the current periodicals display at Holy Cross College's new Science Library. View from the Swords Hall Science Mall. (A Michael J. Novia photo.)

The Libraries of the Los Alamos National Laboratory

Lois Erwin Godfrey

ABSTRACT. The fourth-largest library collection in the state of New Mexico is that of the Los Alamos National Laboratory. Occupied in April 1977, the solar heated and cooled facility which houses the Laboratory's Main and Report Libraries is rapidly filling with one of the most complete science collections in the mountain west. Features of the facility are described.

DESCRIPTION OF THE LIBRARY SYSTEM

The Los Alamos National Laboratory is located at an altitude of 7300 feet in the Jemez Mountains of north-central New Mexico, 35 miles northwest of the State Capitol of Santa Fe. Library and information services are provided to the more than 8,000 employees, of whom 2,500 are scientists and engineers, by the Information Services Division's group IS-4, Library Services. Because the Laboratory itself is spread over 44 square miles, many library users never appear in the Main or Report Libraries. They use telephone and inter-office mail service to request, receive, and return materials, both classified and unclassified, and their branch libraries for access to journals of primary interest. The Main Library is, however, open 24 hours a day, seven days a week to laboratory badgeholders, and to the public from 8:00 am to 4:30 pm on working days.

Forty full-time equivalent employees, about 50 people under the direction of Head Librarian J. Arthur Freed, oper-

---

Lois Erwin Godfrey is Assistant Head Librarian of the Los Alamos National Laboratory, Los Alamos, NM 87545. She attended the University of Michigan, and holds a BS in Library Science from Simmons College.

© 1986 by The Haworth Press, Inc. All rights reserved.

ate the Main Library, Report Library, and 24 branch libraries, the largest of which is the Medical Library. Except for the Medical Library, branch libraries are not staffed by IS-4 employees, but all material in them is acquired and processed by IS-4. Most are run as reference collections by a secretary in the group or division served. The IS-4 staff is organized into five sections: the Group Office, Main Library, Reference, Technical Processes, and Report Library. About half of the staff is assigned to the Technical Processes section.

The collection has major strengths in astronomy, astrophysics, biomedicine, chemistry, energy (including the military and peaceful uses of nuclear energy), engineering, geology, mathematics, and physics.

The library is currently in the process of installing GEAC's automated system to handle acquisitions, circulation, and an online catalog, which will be available to laboratory employees from their office computers. Cataloging has been done with the Research Libraries Information Network, RLIN, for the past six years.

THE FACILITY FOR THE MAIN AND REPORT LIBRARIES: THE J. ROBERT OPPENHEIMER STUDY CENTER

The J. Robert Oppenheimer Study Center (originally called the National Security and Resources Study Center) is a three-level structure of approximately 70,000 square feet connected to the Laboratory's adjacent Administration Building by an enclosed concourse at the upper level. The building houses on the upper level what is known as the "Study Center," which provides basic facilities for special research study groups investigating specific scientific problems of a national or international nature. It is increasingly used for scientific or technical conferences of varying size.

The Main Library is housed on the ground level, and two-thirds of the lower level. The other third of the lower level is a vault, with access through a security station. The vault houses the Laboratory's Report Library of classified and unclassified technical reports.

A striking feature of the building is 8,000 square feet of flat-plate, liquid-heating, solar collectors, especially designed and developed by the Laboratory's solar energy group. These are arranged in an 80 feet wide by 100 feet high south-facing planar array which slopes 35 degrees to the horizontal. Each 2-foot by 10-foot collector combines the functions of roof and solar collector by providing weather exclusion, structural support, thermal insulation, and energy absorption. Approximately 94% of the building's heating requirements and 70% of its cooling demand is provided by the sun.

The building itself is energy-conserving, featuring R-19 insulation, double glazing, floating temperature-humidity setpoints, a heat recovery unit, air-cooled light fixtures, fresh air evaporative cooling, and summer nighttime storage of chilled water from a cooling tower. These features reduce the building's gross thermal load from approximately 7,600 million BTU/yr to 2,100 million BTU/yr.[1]

PLANNING FOR THE FACILITY

The library staff had been formulating ideas for a separate building to house its operations and collections in a low key way for at least the last ten years in its previous Administration Building basement quarters. But funding was an obstacle. J. Arthur Freed addressed this question in detail in a paper[2] delivered to the American Library Association in June 1978. Eventually, through support from New Mexico's Congressional delegation, and especially Senator Joseph M. Montoya, and the (now) Department of Energy on various levels, the approximately $4.6 million required was assured, in 1973.

The Laboratory's Engineering Department was responsible for preparing preliminary designs and specifications for the building, and did that with substantial input from IS-4. Our liaison with the Engineering Department was the building's Project Manager, L.J. (John) Finley, Jr., who was very helpful to us, and cordial. Mr. Freed and I were the library contacts. We became involved early, and stayed as involved as possible. When we learned, occasionally, of a meeting we hadn't been told about, we attended it, uninvited. After the firm of Charles Luckman and Associates was chosen as the architect-engineer for the project, we continued our agressive involvement, and went to design conferences in Los Angeles, as well as attending all Los Alamos meetings, even when the agenda topic was said to be only details of the heating system.

The Library staff was asked for ideas and criticisms at every stage of the design effort, and we worked diligently to make them feel involved.

The third group of Laboratory people involved in this building are mentioned above—the solar energy researchers and people concerned with monitoring and controlling the heating and cooling systems of a radical new design. We answered their endless questions about temperature and humidity requirements, lighting levels, the number of people expected to be in various areas of the building at different times of the day or night, the need for all night lighting, and expected energy-producing equipment such as photocopying machines and computer terminals.

Everyone realized that the budget would not build a structure which could house a rapidly-expanding collection for many years, so the building was designed to accept an addition on the lower level on either the north or east. Funding for an addition has not been available.

LAYOUT AND FEATURES

There is only one entrance to the Main Library. As one enters, there is immediately in view a large circulation desk of white Formica, which is shaped as three quarters of a circle of about 25 feet diameter. Three circulation clerks can work there comfortably at one time. Immediately beyond the circulation desk, to the left (north), one sees the card catalog, and beside that the beginning of the journal display area, where current issues of 1400 journals are displayed on waist-high racks, with seating for 24 readers interspersed. A newspaper reading area with lounge seating is a window alcove beyond the current journals. The rest of the visible open area is taken up with stacks for books with Dewey numbers 001–599, reference journals and reference books, carrel and table seating for 40 readers, and the semi-circular reference desk. The open central stairway to the lower level is also clearly visible.

The entire technical process area is to the right (south) of the circulation desk from the entrance, and is defined by full height, but partial-length walls. The staff room, receiving or mail room, and computer room, as well as the solar gallery and solar equipment are housed along the south side of the building.

The Library/group office, a copying room, and rest rooms are adjacent to the current journal area, on the west side.

The lower floor of the Main Library houses the rest of the book collection (Dewey numbers 600–999) and the entire journal collection except for issues on display. There is a carrel space, and other seating, for about 60 people on this level. There are no partitions of any sort in the stack area of the lower level and the support pillars are on 27 foot centers, so the entire area is visually open. Rest rooms, elevator and electrical equipment, and janitorial storage areas are along the west section of the south wall.

The south wall of the lower floor's Main Library is the north wall of the Report Library's vault. The vault's 7700 square foot space is about two thirds stack space; one third of that is compact shelving. Circulation, reference, and some acquisitions activity is carried on in the non-stack space. Cataloging of all unclassified material is done upstairs in the Technical Processes section. Classified reports and films are cataloged in the vault. Reader space is limited to one table, and two microfiche reader-printers.

COMPROMISES, AND POST-OCCUPANCY CHANGES

The architects convinced us that an open plan would be flexible for work space, as well as for stack space, but when conduits for electricity and telephones are not installed as shown on floor plans, that is untrue. We were not sufficiently far-sighted to realize the greatly increasing demands for electricity and data cabling with which we are now faced.

The open area for stacks and carrels works well, but in work areas it is difficult for supervisors to find a place to talk privately with their subordinates, as in annual performance appraisals, and some people find it hard to concentrate on the detail of their jobs when there is a lot of movement of people and books trucks going on around them constantly. With carpeted floors, the noise level has rarely been a problem, although phone conversations can be overheard at nearby desks. With automation has come the need for more electric lines, and data transmission lines, encased in conduit which now adorns every pillar in the work area, and some pillars in public areas.

Partly because the amount of money for the building was set years before it was built, in an era of great inflation of building costs and scientific journal publishing, the building when occupied allowed space for only 5 years expansion of the collection. Installation of compact shelving and Lektrievers for microfiche storage in the vault and moving, in 1980, of all unclassified reports into that area which was designed initially for only the small classified collection, was a major change, and did allow the book and journal collection to fit into the Main Library's stack areas for almost 9 years.

Originally, a range of stacks was set at each pillar, with 44" aisles and four ranges of stacks between each pair of pillars. In mid-1985 all of the shelving was moved closer to the pillars, aisle width decreased to 33", and the resulting spaces filled in with another range of stacks, so there are now five ranges between each set of pillars. There is about a 20% increase in shelving, but the spacious look is gone. We have recently determined that the 6,234 shelves we now have for the journal collection will be exactly adequate for the present collection plus 5 years expansion of the 4,000 active titles, with 300 shelves available for new titles during that time. Space for the book collection is probably also now adequate for another five years, as the result of the same shelving addition, and a drastic weeding program recently completed. We hope that optical disk or a similar technology will be available to us as we run out of space for shelving bound journals.

HINDSIGHT

The space problem which faces all science-oriented libraries was predicted, but had no solution. We could, however, have been more firm about provision of office space for supervisory personnel, and should have done that. We also should have insisted on some interior walls for telephone, electrical, and data transmission wiring to run in, throughout the technical processes area.

STATISTICS

Gross area	45,000 sq. ft.
Staff size	
Professional	16 fte
Non-professional	24 fte
Seating for users	100 at carrels, tables, etc., plus lounge furniture
Employees served	2,500 scientists and engineers, 5,500 other
Annual circulation	80,000 within the laboratory
Annual budget for collection	$2,000,000
Collection size	
Books and bound periodicals	310,000
Full-size classified reports	160,000
Full-size unclassified reports	200,000
Unclassifed reports on microfiche	350,000
Current periodical titles	4,000
Current periodical subscriptions	8,000
Computer literature searches per year	5,600
Date of completion	April 1977
Special equipment	GEAC computer system with 16 terminals, 4 Lektrievers, 2 RLIN terminals, 7 microfilm/fiche reader-printers, 4 photocopiers, for do-it-yourself and staff use, 19 units of compact shelving, 8 sections each, double faced (1806 shelves), several database-access computers/terminals

REFERENCES

1. Los Alamos Scientific Laboratory. Solar Energy Group. *Solar heating and cooling research at Los Alamos Scientific Laboratory*. Los Alamos: The Laboratory; 1978. 23p. LASL-78-30.

2. Freed, J. Arthur. *The National Security and Resources Study Center: a librarian's overview*. Los Alamos: Los Alamos Scientific Laboratory; 1978. 13p. LA-UR-78-1662.

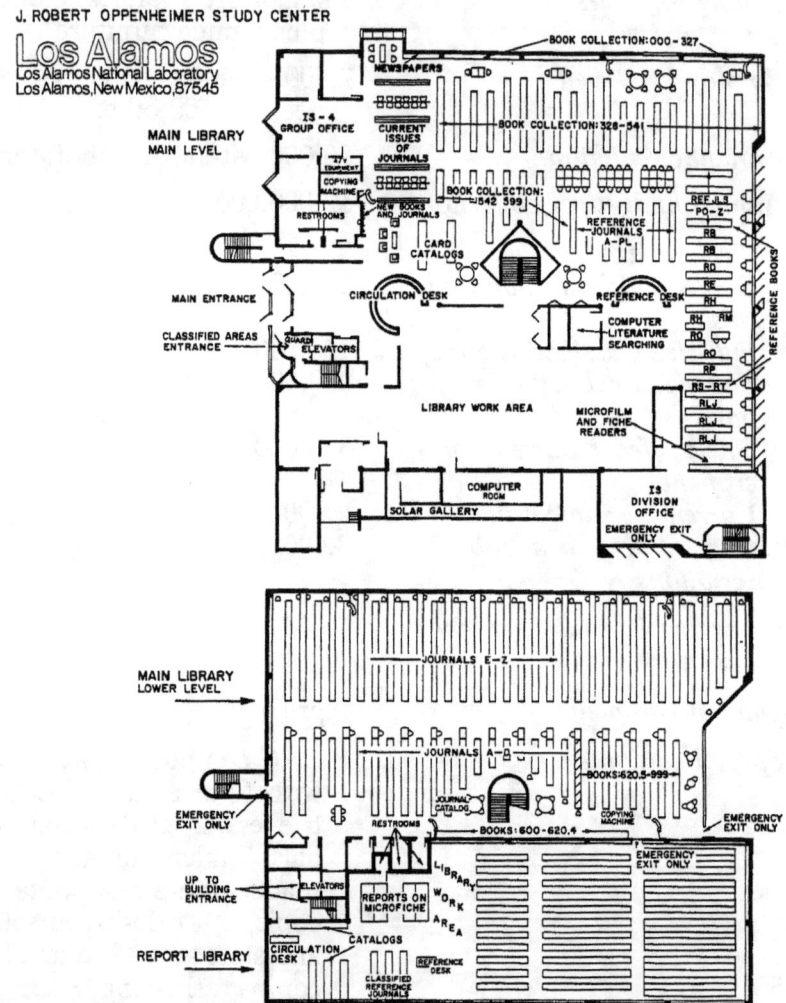

Figure 1

Figure 2

SPECIAL PAPER

Impact of Online Search Services on Special Libraries

Pamela G. Kobelski
Betty Miller

ABSTRACT. This paper reports the results of a survey of 193 New York State special libraries to determine the effects of the online search services on those libraries. The survey indicated that special libraries are heavy users of online search systems and have been for a number of years. While there were changes in library collections there was little evidence of much "print-online migration". The types of databases searched and the use of online systems varied by the subject orientation of the libraries surveyed as did collection and staff size. The amount of end-user searching also varied with the subject orientation. The major impact of online services, outside their effects on library budgets, was to make a number of databases outside their subject areas more easily accessible to special libraries.

Betty Miller is Manager of the Technical Information Center of the Calspan Corporation, P.O. Box 400, Buffalo, NY 14225. She received a Bachelor's degree in physics from the University of Pennsylvania and a Master's degree in Library and Information Science from Drexel University.

Pamela Kobelski is Technical Reference Librarian at AT&T Bell Laboratories in Murray Hill, NJ 07974. She received a Bachelor's degree in chemistry from Northwestern University and a Master's degree in library science from Wayne State University.

INTRODUCTION

The effects of online search systems on libraries has been a frequent literature topic since these systems were first introduced. While an initial survey of all types of libraries by Lancaster[8] indicated few subscriptions were cancelled in favor of online databases, reports from some individual libraries[3,7,15] encourage the replacement of certain subscriptions with online searches. This "print-online migration" has been of great concern to publishers and there have been a number of studies of the affect this has or could have on their revenues.[12,16,17,18,19] We felt the situation, especially for special libraries was more complex than many of the discussions indicated. We conducted a survey of online use by special libraries to try to get a clearer picture of the full impact of online search services on their collections, staff, policies and operations.

SURVEY

A questionnaire to assess this impact was designed. Since the results of this study were to be presented initially at a New York Library Association meeting, we limited our survey to special libraries in New York State. In the summer of 1983 the questionnaire was sent to 193 New York state special libraries listed as using online services in the 8th edition of the *Directory of Special Libraries & Information Centers* (Gale Research 1981). University and hospital libraries and those attached to government agencies were omitted. Replies were received from 92 libraries (47.7% of the libraries surveyed).

LIBRARY DATA

In addition to the survey data, the subject classifications given in the *Directory of Special Libraries & Information Centers* were used. Subject specialties of both the libraries queried and those responding were tabulated. The largest single subject grouping was business-finance with 36.8% of the libraries surveyed and 34.7% of the libraries responding in this group. Science-technology libraries accounted for 24.9% of those surveyed and 30.4% of those responding. Law libraries were 17.6% of the survey group and 18.5% of the group responding. Medical and pharmaceutical libraries made up 5.4% of respondents, publishing 4.4%, social science 3.3% and food-beverage collections 3.3%. These approximate their percentages of the total libraries surveyed. Table 1 shows the subject specialization breakdown of libraries surveyed and those responding.

Special libraries tend to be small; this proved to be true of the group we surveyed. Generally the libraries responding reported between 1 and 3 professional and staff employees. Responses are tabulated in Table 2. However staff size was related to the type of library. Business-finance libraries had an average of 3.6 professionals, law libraries 3.2 and science-technology libraries 2.0. Table 3 shows how the professional staff size varied by type of library. There was a similar variation in the support staff size with business-financial libraries averaging 5.1, law libraries 4.8, and science-technology libraries 3.0. The difference is even greater since one science, and technology library with 14 professionals and 26 staff members contributed significantly to the average. There were so few responses in other subject areas that their averages would mean little.

Table 1

Subject Specialization of Special Libraries Surveyed

Subject Area	% Surveyed	% Responding
Business & Finance	36.8%	34.7%
Science & Technology	24.9%	30.4%
Law	17.6%	18.5%
Medical & Pharmaceutical	6.2%	5.4%
Publishing	4.7%	4.4%
Social Science	5.7%	3.3%
Food & Beverage	3.1%	3.3%

Table 2
Special Library Staffing

	Number of Respondents	% Respondents
Professionals		
None	3	3.3%
1 to 3	63	68.4%
4 to 6	13	14.1%
7 to 9	10	10.9%
more than 10	3	3.3%
Staff Members		
None	6	6.5%
1 to 3	51	55.4%
4 to 6	18	19.6%
7 to 9	6	6.5%
more than 10	11	12.0%

Table 3
Number of Professionals by Type of Library

Professionals	Business & Finance	Law	Science & Technology
none	3.1%	0	3.6%
1 to 3	59.4%	64.7%	85.7%
4 to 6	18.7%	17.6%	3.6%
7 to 9	15.6%	17.6%	3.6%
more than 10	3.1%	0	3.6%

The size of the library collections varied in the number of volumes, but most libraries reported receiving over 200 periodical subscriptions. Interlibrary loan volume seemed rather light, with most libraries reporting less than 50 interlibrary loans per month. Detailed data on collections and interlibrary loans is shown on Table 4. Again these numbers varied by the type of library. Business-finance libraries had small volume collections and large numbers of subscriptions. Law libraries had greater numbers of volumes, but fewer periodical subscriptions. Science-technology libraries also had a large number of periodical subscriptions. Interlibrary loans were heaviest in law and lightest in business and finance. These results are in Table 5.

Since traditionally most special libraries themselves have performed any literature searches needed by their organizations, we asked whether they provided literature searches and/or current awareness services using printed tools as well as online search services. Eighty seven libraries (95.6%) reported that they provided manual literature searches and 65

Table 4

Special Library Collections

	Number of Respondents	% Respondents
Bound Volumes		
less than 1,000	9	9.8%
1,000 to 5,000	23	25.0%
5,000 to 10,000	21	22.8%
10,000 to 25,000	23	25.0%
25,000 to 50,000	9	9.8%
over 50,000 volumes	7	7.6%
Periodical Subscriptions		
less than 100	14	15.2%
100 to 200	22	23.9%
over 200	56	60.9%
Interlibrary Loans per Month		
less than 25	35	38.0%
25 to 50	22	23.9%
50 to 100	10	10.9%
100 to 150	12	13.1%
150 to 200	5	5.4%
over 200	8	8.7%

Table 5

Size of Collection by Type of Library

	Business & Finance	Law	Science & Technology
Bound Volumes			
less than 1,000	25.0%	0	3.5%
1,000 to 5,000	21.9%	0	28.6%
5,000 to 10,000	37.5%	5.9%	25.0%
10,000 to 25,000	9.4%	64.7%	17.9%
25,000 to 50,000	3.1%	11.8%	14.3%
over 50,000 volumes	3.1%	17.6%	10.7%
Periodical Subscriptions			
less than 100	6.3%	35.3%	17.9%
100 to 200	9.4%	35.3%	25.0%
over 200	84.4%	29.4%	57.1%
Interlibrary Loans per Month			
less than 25	43.7%	11.8%	32.1%
25 to 50	31.3%	5.9%	35.7%
50 to 100	9.4%	23.5%	10.7%
100 to 150	15.6%	17.6%	3.6%
150 to 200	0	11.8%	7.1%
over 200	0	29.4%	7.1%

(71.4%) that they offered a current awareness service using manual tools.

ONLINE SEARCHING

We knew that all of the responding libraries were actively searching online, but we were surprised at the length of time some had been searching. Eleven libraries reported over 10 years experience with online searching and 58 over 5 years searching. Table 6 shows the length of time reported. The number of years libraries had been searching online did not vary with the type of library. Each of the main types averaged between 5 and 6 years of online searching experience.

There was a wide variation in the average number of connect hours per month that the libraries reported using. (Table 7.) While 15.5% reported using only 5 hours or less per month, 17.6% reported using over 50. Thirty and seven-tenths percent were in the middle with 10 to 25 hours. In addition to having used online services for an extended period

Table 6

Years Experience Searching Online Systems

Years	Number	%
less than 2	1	1.1%
2 years	8	8.7%
3 years	14	15.2%
4 years	11	12.0%
5 years	15	16.2%
6 years	8	8.7%
7 years	9	9.8%
8 years	12	13.0%
9 years	3	3.3%
10 years	8	8.7%
over 10 years	3	3.3%

Table 7

Connect Hours per Month Used for Online Searching

	Number	%
Less than 5 hours per month	15	16.5%
5 to 10 hours per month	16	17.6
10 to 25 hours per month	28	30.7
25 to 50 hours per month	16	17.6%
50 to 100 hours per month	9	9.9%
over 100 hours per month	7	7.7%

of time, the libraries surveyed are also frequent searchers. Again there were no differences between the types of libraries in the number of connect hours used per month.

We also asked libraries about the type of online search services they used. We used catagories of General, Data Banks, Information and Full Text. General services were defined as those offering both bibliographic and nonbibliographic databases such as DIALOG, BRS, SDC, NLM and Pergamon. Informational services included Compuserve, Dow Jones, and the Source. Data banks were defined as strictly nonbibliographic files, e.g., Chase Econometrics, I.P. Sharp, and Chemical Information Systems. Full-text services included LEXIS, NEXIS and WESTLAW. Results for all respondents and by type of library are given in Table 8. The type of online services used varied considerably by the type of library with business-finance libraries heavy users of all four types of services, law libraries heavy users of informational and full text services, and science-technology libraries heavy users of general and data bank services.

Subject searching is generally considered to be the primary use for online services. We also asked about their use for other purposes. Their use for full text searching and current awareness was not too surprising. The 53.3% using such services to manipulate data indicates the importance of non-bibliographic databases to special libraries. Breaking down responses by type of library showed that data manipulation was generally done by business-finance or science-technology

Table 8

Type of Online Search Services Used

	General	Data Banks	Informational	Full Text
All libraries				
Number	83	15	53	52
%	90.2%	16.3%	57.6%	56.5%
Business & Finance	93.8%	31.3%	81.3%	75.0%
Law	64.7%	0	70.6%	100.0%
Science & Technology	96.4%	14.3%	35.7%	21.4%

libraries. The capability to order documents online was being used by 44.6% of our respondents. The surprisingly low number of interlibrary loans reported is probably caused by this sort of usage. This is at least suggested by the fact that the types of libraries with the lower reported rates of interlibrary loan (business-finance and science-technology) report the greatest use of online services for document ordering. One library, in fact, reported that all requests that previously would have been interlibrary loans are ordered online from commercial sources when feasible. Only 14.1% used private files capabilities offered by some services, with a large percentage of these being legal libraries. This data is given in Table 9.

Although special library collections were concentrated in only a few subject areas, their online utilization covered a number of databases with 8.7% reporting searching over 100 different databases in a year (see Table 10). Again there was little difference in the number of data bases used between the various types of libraries. Most libraries could not possibly subscribe to the print versions of all, or even most, of the databases they reported searching.

We also asked about policies for charging back to departments or individuals for library services. While all funds are still coming from the corporate budget, online searching has an easily identified cost attached and therefore may be handled differently. Over half the libraries responding (59.8%) charged for online searches, while 39.1% charged back for one or more manual library services. Table 11 details the variety of services involving charges. Charging patterns were similar for the different types of libraries.

End user searching is becoming a frequently discussed topic in the library field. We asked libraries if they allowed end-user searching and 25 (27.2%) replied that they did while 45 (48.9%) reported end-user searching within their organization. End user searching varied considerably by type of library, with 94.1% of the law libraries reporting they allowed user searching as opposed to only 9.4% of the business libraries and 17.9% of science-technology libraries. Of the business-finance libraries, 68.6% reported end user searching elsewhere in their organizations as opposed to 41.4% of the law libraries and 39.3% of the science-technology libraries. With

Table 9
Other Uses of Online Services

	Number	%
Current Awareness	46	50.0%
Document Ordering	41	44.6%
Private Files	13	14.1%
Full Text	59	64.1%
Data Manipulation	49	53.3%

By Type of Library	Business & Finance	Law	Science & Technology
Current Awareness	40.6%	35.3%	67.9%
Document Ordering	56.3%	5.9%	67.9%
Private Files	12.5%	29.4%	10.7%
Full Text	68.8%	100.0%	46.4%
Data Manipulation	50.0%	35.3%	60.7%

Table 10
Number of Data Bases Searched per Year

	Number	%
Less than 10 data bases	18	19.6%
10 to 25 data bases	32	34.8%
25 to 50 data bases	17	18.5%
50 to 100 data bases	16	17.4%
over 100 data bases	8	8.7%

the increased use of personal computers, end user searching will probably become more common.

ONLINE SEARCHING AND PRINT SUBSCRIPTIONS

"Print-online migration", cancelling a printed index or abstract and using its online equivalent, has become a major fear of publishers. We asked libraries what percentage of their searching was done in the online equivalents of printed indexes or abstracts to which they subscribed. This data appears in Table 12. Over half of the libraries (51.7%) reported that 25% or less of their searching was done in online equivalents of library subscriptions. The percentages did not vary by the type of library.

To get some measure of what effect online search services have had on special libraries, we asked if they had cancelled or added subscriptions to indexes or abstracts since starting online searching. We asked the percentage of the indexes or abstracts cancelled or added that were available to them for online searching. We then asked them what importance the availability of indexes or abstracts online had to their decision to add or cancel. The results, by type of library, appear in Table 13. While more libraries had added subscriptions than had cancelled, the cancellation rate was quite high in science-technology libraries. This is probably due to the increase in price of scientific literature in the past few years. For most

Table 11

Library Charges

	Number	%
Charges for Online Searches	55	59.8
Charges for Other Library Services	36	39.1%
Interlibrary Loans	26	28.3%
Manual Searches	23	25.0%
Document Ordering	22	23.9%
Manual Current Awareness	12	13.0%

Table 12

Searches in Online Equivalents to Library Subscriptions

	Number	%
Less than 25% in online equivalents	45	51.7%
25% to 50% in online equivalents	22	25.3%
50% to 75% in online equivalents	16	18.4%
over 75% in online equivalents	4	4.6%

Table 13
Influence of Online Services on Cancel/Add Decisions

	Index Abstracts Cancelled	Index Abstracts Added
Total % of libraries	45.7%	52.2%
Business & Finance	37.5%	56.3%
Law	17.7%	47.1%
Science & Technology	64.3%	50.0%
% Indexes or Abstracts Available Online		
less than 25%	20.9%	82.3%
25% to 50%	34.9%	4.4%
50% to 75%	12.4%	4.4%
over 75%	32.8%	8.9%
Importance of Availability of Online Equivalent to Decision to Add or Cancel		
Important	70.3%	56.1%
Minor consideration	18.9%	19.5%
Not a factor	10.8%	24.4%

libraries the availability of an online equivalent was important in their cancellation decision. It was less important in deciding whether to add a subscription. Cancelling and adding subscriptions to indexes and abstracts is a common occurrence in special libraries. In many cases it is a result of changes in company structure, products or goals. When one of our companies decided to cease producing edible vegetable oils, subscriptions to agricultural and nutritional materials were dropped. This was before online services were available. Having materials available online is excellent for reassurance, but would have had little impact on the decision to drop materials that were no longer needed.

OVERALL EFFECTS ON SPECIAL LIBRARIES

We asked a number of questions to try to assess the overall impact of online search services on special libraries. Answers to these questions are tabulated in Table 14. The answers suggest the online services have had greater impact on staff and collections in business-finance libraries while their impact on budget was greater in law and science-technology libraries.

Comments Received on Online Search Services

A number of comments we received in response to the questionnaire bring out important points.

Online services provide "access to information sources which would otherwise be prohibitively expensive for our size; we gain the ability to provide reference assistance in any subject area when our collection is primarily technical." The large number of databases used and the low percentage of these available in libraries in print form suggest that special libraries use online databases to supplement, not to replace, print subscriptions. This is in line with results found by others.[2,6,11,14] When materials are not available in the library or online, it doesn't mean that they are not used. As one librarian noted; online searching ". . . cuts the amount of time spent traveling to various special libraries and searching indexes manually . . .". Special libraries

Table 14

Question	% Yes All Libraries	% Yes Bus. Fin.	% Yes Law	% Yes Sci. Tech.
Significant change in collection size	29.0%	21.9%	23.5%	39.3%
Were online services responsible	42.9%	57.1%	0	45.0%
Significant change in staff size	35.9%	34.3%	23.5%	42.8%
Were online services responsible	33.3%	36.4%	25.0%	25.0%
Have online services impacted library budgets	55.0%	40.6%	52.9%	67.9%

use public and university libraries to access materials needed only occasionally. This would mean no additional revenue for print index publishers. By placing databases online, searching becomes more convenient for libraries and opens additional sources of revenue for database publishers.

The availability of full text databases has also been an asset to special libraries. "There is no longer a wait for documents that have been ordered orally such as slip opinions."

The overall impact of online search services was summed up by one librarian; "I would have had to have added another librarian and spent far more on reference materials without them."

SUMMARY OF SURVEY RESULTS

Overall our survey indicated that our sample of New York State special libraries are heavy users of online search services. They have been using such services for a number of years and use them for other purposes in addition to subject searching. While the availability of an online database definitely seems to influence a library's decision to cancel a publication, we found no evidence of wholesale migration. In fact, much searching is done in databases to which the library does not have an equivalent subscription. Most libraries felt online searching has had an impact on their budgets and most reported charging back online search costs. Online searching has made many information resources much more accessible for special libraries and has undoubtedly saved them a great deal of time and money. Most forecasters[4,5,10,13] see greater numbers of online databases available for library use. They also predict an increase in end user searching. These two trends are already evident in the libraries we surveyed.

BIBLIOGRAPHY

1. Baldinger, Ester L.; et al. An experimental study of the feasibility of substituting Chemical Abstracts on-line for the printed copy in a medium-sized medical library. *Bulletin of the Medical Library Association.* 69(2): 247–251; 1981 April.

> Baldinger relates a study at Washington University School of Medicine that considered substituting *Chemical Abstracts* online for the

print subscription. The conclusion reached was not to substitute because: (1) while formulating strategies for online searching, the paper copy was used; (2) most patrons wanted to see the abstracts; (3) patrons wanted to browse; (4) older years were required.

2. Chambers, John. A scientist's view of print versus online. *ASLIB Proceedings*. 36 (7/8): 309–316; 1984 July/August.

In this paper Chambers gives some advantages and disadvantages of both online and print versions from the viewpoint of a scientist end-user. Chambers concludes that if some of the disadvantages associated with online could be improved, subscriptions could be dropped. One advantage mentioned by Chambers that is frequently cited is the availability of sources outside the primary interest of the library. Very few libraries can afford to subscribe to all the sources that are available to them online.

3. Childs, Susan; Carmel, Michael. Effect of online services on purchases of a printed index. *ASLIB Proceedings*. 33(9): 351–356; 1981 September.

Childs relates a study considering not one library, but a regional group of 16 libraries. A survey was taken to determine if the availability of MEDLINE had influenced the purchase of *Index Medicus*. The results state: "We have found that the availability of MEDLINE has not adversely affected the purchase and use of *Index Medicus*. The purchase of *Index Medicus* has continued to rise and the availability of MEDLINE has in fact had a positive effect on its use." This finding may be peculiar to the *Index Medicus* which is relatively inexpensive and easy to use compared with tools such as *Chemical Abstracts*. This may make it less vulnerable to competition from its own online version.

4. Clayton, Audrey. Factors affecting future online services. *Online Review*. 5(4): 287–300; 1981.

This paper discusses the future of online services and the development of online databases without print equivalents.

5. Dougherty, Richard M; Lougee, Wendy P. What will survive? *Library Journal*. 110(2): 41–44; 1985 February.

Another discussion of what the future holds for online search services.

6. Garfield, Eugene. Online and print information services are not always equivalent for all users. *Database.* 3(3): 4–6; 1980 September.

> In this guest editorial Garfield states ". . .Online enthusiasts have no right to deprive users of the benefits of printed indexes. The print versions of the *Science Citation Index* and the *Social Science Citation Index* offer easy access to information to everyone—both library staff and library patrons." He also mentions the browsability of printed indexes.

7. Herring, Mark Y. Online databases vs. hard copy subscriptions. *Library Hi Tech.* 1(1): 63–68; 1983 Summer.

> Herring tells of dropping several abstract and index subscriptions and replacing them with online services when the King College Library had to cut its budget. For two of these sources, a year's worth of searching cost $1700 as opposed to $5000 for printed copies. He also mentions the advantage of having access to a wide variety of files and quotes a senior member of the faculty's appreciation of having access to "a file he had always wanted but the library was never able to afford."

8. Lancaster, F. Wilfrid; Goldhor, Herbert. The impact of online services on subscriptions to printed publications. *Online Review.* 5(4): 301–311; 1981 August.

> This paper reports the results of a survey covering 164 libraries of various types. The libraries held a total of 2168 subscriptions to abstracting and indexing services. Of these 102 were cancelled but in 58.8% of the cases online availability did not influence the decision to cancel. Thus cancellations even partially influenced by online availability account for only 2% of library subscriptions. Lancaster remarks that while database producers may be losing money from print subscriptions, they are gaining from online revenues. This paper notes many new libraries are utilizing online resources without ever having had the printed equivalents.

9. Lancaster, F. Wilfrid; Neway, Julie M. The future of abstracting and indexing services. *Journal of the American Society for Information Science.* 33(3): 183–189; 1982 May.

> Lancaster, in discussing the future of abstracting and indexing services, mentions the advantages of online searching. In particular, he says "It makes a much wider range of information resources available to more libraries. Thus, a small industrial library that a decade ago subscribed to only four or five secondary services, and had to rely almost entirely on these to support literature searching activities, now finds itself with well over 100 databases readily accessible. To sub-

scribe to all of these in printed form (assuming all existed in this form) would be out of the question. In the electronic environment, a database needed once a year is no less accessible than one needed once a week. This is quite untrue of the print-on-paper situation, where subscription to a publication (and therefore access to it) can only be justified if a reasonable volume of use can be anticipated."

10. Lancaster, Frederick W. The evolving paperless society and its implications for libraries. *International Forum for Information and Documentation.* 7(7): 3–10; 1982.

Lancaster discusses the emergence of electronic databases and the probable increase in end-user searching. He states, "It would be true to say that, particularly in special libraries, online access to remote sources is already more important for the literature searching activity than the use of print-on-paper sources within the library itself."

11. Neely, Glenda S. Online databases: effects on reference acquisitions. *Library Acquisitions: Practice and Theory.* 5(1): 45–49; 1981.

Neely gives an overview of the print versus online questions and concludes that little-used, expensive sources can be accessed online rather than via hard copies.

12. Neufeld, M. Lynne. Future of secondary services. *Online Review.* 7(5): 421–426; 1983.

Neufeld in discussing the future of secondary services brings up a new point. "Outside of the U.S., Western Europe and Japan, the vast majority of users will continue to rely on print as being the only source for information transfer and dissemination available to them. Overseas subscriptions represent 50% or more of the sales for the major secondary service producers."

13. Newcomb, J. Electronic information distribution: the role of the traditional publisher and the librarian. *Special Libraries.* 74(2): 150–155; 1983 April.

A view of the future of online databases.

14. Norton, Tom. Secondary publications have a future in libraries. *ASLIB Proceedings.* 36(7/8): 317–323; 1984.

Norton looks at the advantages and disadvantages from a librarian's viewpoint. He specifically mentions the difficulty in browsing with an online database and the fact that online access is not as readily available to everyone as printed sources are. He also stresses that libraries are not going to cancel subscriptions to those services that are fundamental to their organization's work.

15. Pfaffenberger, Ann; Echt, Sandy. Substitution of SCISEARCH and SOCIAL SCISEARCH for their print versions in an academic library (and the effects of the new SCISEARCH rates). *Database*. 3(1): 63–71; 1980 March.

At Texas Christian University a study was done with *Science Citation Index* and *Social Science Citation Index*. Pfaffenberger says, "Online access might prove cost-effective when considered as an alternative to the purchase of an expensive print index that is important but lightly used . . . that is, there was reason to believe that online searching would produce the same or better results than manual searching in less time at less cost to T.C.U." This library decided to cancel *Science Citation Index* but keep *Social Science Citation Index* due to the different usage patterns of each.

16. Sperr, Inez L. Online searching and the print product: impact or interaction? *In:* Proceedings of the Online Information Meeting. Held December 7–9, 1982 in London, England. 1982. Available from: the author, Migration Information & Abstracts Service, 294 Bunker Hill Road, Orangeburg, NY 10962.

Sperr reports a survey taken of 15 members of the National Federation of Abstracting and Indexing Services. "The picture that emerged showed that various types of printed publications were affected differently, and that there has been 2–5% annual attrition in subscriptions to printed publications over the past five years but it is not related solely or primarily to the availability of online databases, and, that the evolution of online databases and printed publications as separate and distinct entities is accelerating . . . rather than 'impact' of online on print, there is an interaction of the two in a dynamic environment."

17. Trubkin, Loene. Migration from print to online use. *Online Review*. 4(1): 5–12; 1980 March.

Trubkin examines the economics of publishing information services and the effects of migration on profitability. She concludes, " . . .to the extent that migration occurs and printed services become less healthy, online charges by the database publisher are likely to increase."

18. Williams, Martha E. Relative impact of print and databse products on database producer expenses and income—trends for database producer organizations based on a thirteen year financial analysis. *Information Processing and Management* (England). 17(5): 263–276; 1981.

19. Williams, Martha E. Relative impact of print and database products on database producer expenses and income—a follow-up. *Information Processing and Management* (England). 18(6): 307–311; 1982.

> Williams' two studies look at the financial aspects of print/online. She says, "Online use of the database is increasing as is income from online use, but at the same time profit is decreasing and the number of subscriptions to print products is decreasing. The decrease in subscriptions may be the result of any one or a combination of the following: price increases for print products, budget decreases in the subscriber organizations, migration or other reasons." and "The decrease in subscription income must be compensated for by an increase in revenue from online use."

SCI-TECH COLLECTIONS

Tony Stankus, Editor

The collection development paper for this issue covers a very important topic, namely laser science and technology. This study of the literature, by Emerson Hilker, is a fine example of a compact but thorough review of both printed literature and online databases devoted to the laser, a device that has revolutionized many segments of our society, such as communication, medical practice, manufacturing methods, etc. The paper also lists important organizations involved with lasers.

Information Sources in Laser Science and Technology

Emerson Hilker

ABSTRACT. A healthy industry has evolved around the application of lasers in materials processing, communications, medicine, information storage and retrieval, graphic arts, scientific research and development, metrology, remote sensing and even entertainment. These applications have resulted from twenty-five years of research and development recorded in an ever-increasing body of scientific and technical literature, which is discussed in this collection development paper. Sections include subject background and future developments, and lists of periodicals, research reports, monographs and monographic series, published bibliographies, abstracting, indexing and current awareness services, as well as an inventory of some laboratories currently pursuing research and applications.

BACKGROUND

The Laser

The laser, one of the most intriguing of the post-World War II creations has spent much of its early life as an invention seeking a significant application, or as one author puts its, a solution looking for a problem![1] The first laser device, invented by T. H. Maiman, appeared to the public eye as the incarnation of the deadly high energy or death rays of fictional fame.[2] To date that threat has not come to practical realization though several world powers are mounting significant research projects to bring the military application of laser systems to a reality. It is in the scientific and industrial arenas

---

Emerson Hilker is Head of the Science and Engineering Library at the Wayne State University Libraries, Detroit, MI 48202. He received his BS and MLS degrees from the University of Illinois-Urbana.

© 1986 by The Haworth Press, Inc. All rights reserved.

that lasers have blossomed into an important tool to accomplish a wide variety of precise tasks. Indeed, the market for laser-related systems mushroomed in 1983 to well over three billion dollars. The government alone generated projects in research and development totaling 800 million dollars.[3] In turn the industrial sector injected another 200 million dollars into laser R&D. The government's continued interest in large scale military projects and the explosive growth of new applications bodes well for the future growth of the market for laser devices of all kinds.

The laser is a device for generating a very narrow, highly directional intense beam of light in the range from submillimeter through ultraviolet and x-ray wave lengths.[4] Characteristics of lasers that make it unique are

1. The laser generates a beam of coherent light, highly suitable for communication purposes.
2. The laser generates high power from a small power supply.
3. The laser produces a very narrow, line-of-sight, straight beam of energy.
4. The laser beam can focus all of its energy on an extremely small point.

Most of the lasers applied commercially today were invented in the 1960's. Through concentrated development and resulting refinements, older devices have become highly marketable. There are four general classes of lasers classified according to the medium in which they operate: gas, liquid, insulated solid, semiconductor.[5]

Gas Lasers

The earliest gas laser, Helium-Neon invented in 1962 is still heavily used in many commercial markets due to its relative low cost, reliability and compact size. H-N lasers are in favor where a straight-line source is needed for measurement, inspection, alignment and similar uses. Sales of H-N instruments should approach 30 million dollars in 1985.[6]

The ion laser, another instrument utilizing gas as a medium was invented two years later. Ion lasers have found favor in graphics and high-speed printer applications. Sales of ion devices should reach 82 million dollars in 1985. Carbon-dioxide (CO_2) lasers first appeared in 1964 at Bell Laboratories. The CO_2 laser demonstrated not only high power capabilities, but also great flexibility in all power ranges. This device is useful in metal working applications where concentrated high power is needed and at the other end of the spectrum in medical service where low power and compactness is important. Applications in research and military sectors are commonplace as well. CO_2 lasers will capture the highest percentage of the market, about 115 million dollars in 1985. The increase since 1984 will also be the most dramatic, about 30%. Excimer lasers have come onto the scene relatively late (1975) but are expected to have wide application because of their high power and short wavelength characteristics. Uses have been found in most market sectors. Excimer lasers should gross 19 million dollars in 1985.

Liquid Lasers

Liquid lasers are of two types: Pulsed dye first used in 1966 and continuous-wave introduced in 1970. An organic dye solution is utilized as the medium. Most dye lasers are pumped by another laser such as a nitrogen, neodymium garnet or excimer laser. Dye lasers are desired for their versatility and flexibility and are in demand for spectroscopy applications. Dye laser sales are expected to total 19 million dollars in 1985.

Solid State Lasers: Insulator

Solid state lasers are particularly useful in materials processing applications. The ruby laser, the father of all laser types was invented in 1960 and is still in use for drilling tasks. The neodymium garnet laser first set to work in 1964 possesses material processing capabilities for cutting, welding and drilling. Neodymium glass devices find uses in both scientific research and material processing; especially drilling and welding. Alexandrite, first applied in 1977, has great potential for air-pollution monitoring, rangefinders and material processing. Solid state lasers will capture about 25% of the market or about 100 million dollars in 1985, second only to the CO_2 laser.

Solid State Lasers: Semiconductor

Semicondutor diode lasers, uniquely small and highly efficient devices, are becoming increasingly important in fiber optic communications, reprographics, information handling and process control. One type, the turntable diode laser, is used extensively in spectroscopy. Seventy-nine million dollars in sales is expected for 1985.

FUTURE DEVELOPMENTS

General Considerations

In all commercial areas of application unit cost will be the most critical factor and those devices such as the diode laser that can reduce production costs can be expected to improve their share of the market. Other demands from would-be purchasers include:

1. Compact size without loss of power.
2. More deliverable power without increase in size.
3. Reliability and long-life.

Laser devices should benefit from research and development efforts, especially, those generated by the federal government.

Material Processing

Material processing applications account for the largest demand on laser devices. The laser has been found to be more efficient than traditional methods for most operations involving cutting, welding, heat treating, etching and drilling.[7] The laser is cleaner, more mobile and can be combined with machine control technology.[8] Robot arms and laser heads can be integrated nicely into flexible manufacturing systems.[9]

Dramatic growth in the blending of these high tech areas can be expected. In the electronics industry new laser types will be used in high-density patterning, reflow soldering and wire stripping operations.

Communications

Lasers may well have their greatest impact in communications where light beams can carry all forms of frequency transmission on glass fibers smaller in diameter than the human hair. This increase in scale of efficiency will revolutionize the industry.

Medicine

In the field of medicine the application of lasers in surgery has become commonplace. The laser scalpel can cut more precisely and result in less damage to tissue.[10] Lasers can weld bleeding vessels in the retina, treat aneurysms and remove arterial plaque.[11] Surgeons will want more "user-friendly" models that are reliable and small enough to be hand-held. Experimentation in photoradiation therapy and photoablative surgery will continue.[12,13] Multipurpose lasers capable of cutting on the one hand while being able to induce coagulation on the other hand can increase the surgeon's efficiency.

Information Processing and Graphic Arts

The growth of electronic publishing and office-automation equipment is spurring the demand for more laser devices for use in these systems. Commercial barcode reading demands will certainly increase, resulting in greater need for the appropriate laser equipment. Lasers can be expected to play an increasing role as information storage technology advances. As disk player system sales increase, so will the need for more diode lasers.

Alignment, Measurement and Control

The need for lasers in straight-line tasks or very high precision measurements, as small as one hundredth of the diameter of an atom will certainly increase. Lasers will measure remotely, chemical composition, temperature or pressure from satellites.[14,15,16] Interferometry and holographic inspection techniques will receive increased attention in future laser design.[17]

Scientific R&D

The newer and more experimental excimer and free electron lasers are under consideration for military defense needs, where the delivery of high energy to a target over long distances is required.[18] Although 2 billion dollars have already been spent to develop a protective laser weapon system, an effective design has not materialized so far.[19] As rangefinders and designators, lasers do have a military function. Lasers may even be able to beam energy to remote space stations more economically than the stations could produce for themselves.[20] Scientific research needs for a wide variety of high precision, high performance lasers will persist.

Of the 465 millions to be realized from laser sales the major employment will occur in processing materials, nearly 140 million dollars. R&D should rank second at 100 million and medical at 68 million. Graphic arts, communications, information processing, metrology and entertainment follow in that order.

LASER LITERATURE

Whereas the laser was once viewed as an exotic instrument pursuing relevancy, now scientists and engineers are identifying problems where the laser can be the answer. The resulting increase in laser research has generated a burgeoning literature for reporting the results of those inquiries. Journal articles, conference papers, patents, government reports and trade literature on laser science and technology appear with considerable regularity. The accumulation of knowledge has grown to significant proportions, resulting in the formation of a substantive bibliography of research and educational literature, including a scholarly history.

Periodicals

Typically, the bulk of primary literature on lasers is found in scientific, technical and trade journals. These articles appear in a variety of published journals, both by type and subject. Characteristically, the majority of laser papers of a research nature appear in a small core of basic titles. A good physics library should be subscribing to all of them. The list is ordered high to low according to the number of articles appearing in 1983/84.

Soviet Journal of Quantum Electronics.
 English translation of Kvantovaya Elektronika, New York: American Institute of Physics, v.1- ; 1971- .

IEEE Journal of Quantum Electronics.
 New York: Institute of Physics, v.1- ; 1962- .

Electronics Letters.
 London: Institution of Electrical Engineers, vol. 1- ; 1965- .

Optics Communications.
 Amsterdam: North Holland Publishing Co., vol. 1- ; 1969- .

Journal of Applied Physics.
 New York: American Institute of Physics, v.1- ; 1931- .

Applied Physics B: Photophysics and Laser Chemistry.
 New York: Springer-Verlag., v.1- ; 1962- .

Applied Optics.
 New York: American Institute of Physics, v.1- ; 1962- .

Japanese Journal of Applied Physics.
 Tokyo: Japan Society of Applied Physics, v.1- ; 1962- .

Optics Letters.
 New York: American Institute of Physics, v.1- ; 1977- .

Those libraries wishing to further concentrate in the laser field should subscribe to some or all of the specialized literature listed here.

International Journal of Infrared and Millimeter Waves.
 New York: Plenum, v.1- ; 1980- .

Instruments and Experimental Techniques.
English Translation of Pribory: Tekhnika Eksperimenta, New York: Plenum, v.1- ; 1958- .

Journal of Applied Spectroscopy.
English Translation of *Zhurnal Prikladnoi Spektroskopii*, New York: Plenum, v.1- ; 1965- .

Journal of Lightwave Technology.
New York: Institute of Electrical and Electronics Engineers, v.1- ; 1983- .

Journal of Optical Communications.
Berlin: Fachverlag Schiele & Schoen, v.1- ; 1980- .

Journal of Physics E: Scientific Instruments.
Bristol: Institute of Physics, v.1- ; 1923- .

Journal of Soviet Laser Research.
New York: Consultants Bureau, v.1- ; 1980- .

Journal of the Optical Society of America B: Optical Physics.
New York: American Institute of Physics, v.1- ; 1984- .

Laser and Particle Beams.
Cambridge: Cambridge University Press, v.1- ; 1983- .

Laser Chemistry.
New York: Harwood Academic Publishers, v.1- .

Laser Focus.
Littleton: Advanced Technology Publications, v.1- ; 1965- .

Laser Report Newsletter.
Littleton: Advanced Technology Publications.

Laser and Optoelektronik.
Stuttgart: AT Fachverlag, v.1- ; 1969- .

Lasers and Applications.
Torrance: High Tech Publications, v.1- ; 1982- .

Lasers in Surgery and Medicine.
New York: Alan R. Liss, v.1- ; 1980- .

Measurement Techniques.
English Translation of *Izmeritel'naya Tekhnika*, New York: Plenum, v.1- ; 1958- .

Medical Instrumentation.
Arlington: Association for the Advancement of Medical Instrumentation, v.1- ; 1967- .

Optical Engineering.
  Bellingham: Society of Photo-Optical Instrumentation Engineers, v.1- ; 1956- .

Optics and Laser Technology.
  Guldford: Batterworth, v.1- ; 1968- .

Optics and Lasers in Engineering.
  Barking: Elsevier, v.1- ; 1980- .

Optics and Quantum Electronics.
  London: Chapman and Hall, v.1- ; 1969- .

Optics and Spectroscopy.
  English Translation of Optika; Spektrokopiya, New York: Consultants Bureau, v.1- ; 1959- .

Photonics Spectra.
  Pittsfield: Optical Publishing Company, v.1- ; 1967- .

Review of Scientific Instruments.
  New York: American Institute of Physics, v.1- ; 1930- .

Soviet Journal of Optical Technology.
  English Translation of *Optiko-Mekhanicheskaya Promyshlennost,* New York: American Institute of Physics, v.1- ; 1966- .

Laser Focus, Laser Report Newsletter and *Lasers and Applications* are trade journals providing up-to-date information in marketing, business, finance and research in the field of laser technology. Regular features include reports on the federal scene, new technology, an economic forecast and review, and new products. *Laser Focus* regularly reports the availability of trade literature, including handbooks, dictionaries, catalogs, reports, brochures and data sheets. Often the literature is free.

General periodicals such as *Science, New Scientist,* and *High Technology* regularly chronicle new advancements in laser science and technology.

RESEARCH REPORTS AND PATENTS

Research reports constitute a significant albeit less refined portion of the primary literature. Unclassified reports, the consequence of United States government R&D projects, are available from the National Technical Information Service (NTIS).

Classified reports, those bearing on national security, are distributed only to those with appropriate security clearance. NTIS also purveys government-owned patents, translations, analyses and bibliographies in addition to research reports. The government research and development effort with regard to lasers, especially for military applications, has been and may increasingly be significant.

Patents are a unique form of primary literature in that a description of the invention and its application may only appear in this form of publication. Now laser devices may be screened by scanning Class 372 in the Electrical section of the *Official Gazette*. *Chemical Abstracts* and the *Journal of Current Laser Abstracts* are additional sources for seeking out new devices. Examples of new United States patents include:

Controlled-Linewidth Laser Source.
    U.S. Navy. U.S. Patent 4,503,541.

Gain Tuned Laser Resonator.
    Westinghouse Electric. U.S. Patent 4,502,144.

Laser Drilling System Utilizing Photoacoustic Feedback.
    IBM Corp. U.S. Patent 4,504,727.

Power Supply for a Laser.
    Coherent, Inc. U.S. Patent 4,502,145.

Ring Laser Gyro System.
    Honeywell, Inc. U.S. Patent 4,504,146.

MONOGRAPHS AND MONOGRAPHIC SERIES

In the last two decades the volume of monographic literature on laser science and technology has grown substantially. A representative list of recent publications is annotated below to illustrate the wide variety of texts and treatises available:

> Bertolli, M. *Masers and Lasers: an Historical approach.* London: Hilger; 1983. A history of these devices from Einstein's theory through the free electron laser, written for the researcher.

Duley, W. W. *Laser Processing and Analysis of Materials.* New York: Plenum; 1983. An introduction to the application of lasers to material processing.

Earnshaw, J. C. and Steer, M. W. *The Application of Laser Light Scattering to the Study of Biological Motion.* New York: Plenum; 1983. Contains papers of a conference on the application of light scattering techniques to molecular studies. Constitutes a reference for the biophysicist.

Evans, Ted R. *Applications of Lasers to Chemical Problems.* Techniques of Chemistry, 17. New York: Wiley-Interscience; 1982. A review with extensive bibliography for the chemist.

Hecht, Jeff *Beam Weapons: the Next Arms Race.* New York: Plenum; 1984. A detailed and well-referenced survey of the proposed weapon systems utilizing lasers and particle beams. For the nontechnical reader.

Hitz, C. B. *Understanding Laser Technology.* Tulsa: Penn-Well Books; 1985. A nontechnical introduction to lasers for students, scientists in other fields and others interested in obtaining a basic understanding of the field.

Koebner, H. *Industrial Applications of Lasers.* New York: Wiley-Interscience; 1984. Discusses applications of the newest laser techniques to a wide variety of industries. For the student or engineer.

Maeda, M. *Laser Dyes: Properties of Organic Compounds for Dye Lasers.* New York: Academic; 1984. An index of organic compounds used for laser dyes. Dye lasers have a wide variety of uses in science and engineering. A technical reference for the researcher.

Marshall, Thomas C. *Free Electron Lasers.* New York: Macmillan; 1985. The first book on the subject of FELs, lasers whose characteristics include operating efficiency, high power and durability. For the technical reader.

Measures, Raymond M. *Laser Remote Sensing.* New York: Wiley-Interscience; 1984. A graduate text containing an extensive bibliography on the subject.

Rhodes, C. K. ed. *Excimer Lasers.* 2nd ed. New York: Springer-Verlag; 1984. For one of the fast developing laser sources this is the only technical reference.

Shimoda, K. *Introduction to Laser Physics.* New York: Springer-Verlag; 1984. A comprehensive introduction to the field for physics majors.

Sliney, David and Walbarsht, Myren *Safety with Lasers and Other Optical Sources: a Comprehensive Handbook.* New York: Plenum; 1980. Contains a wealth of material on laser safety.

Stenholm, S. *Foundations of Laser Spectroscopy.* New York: Wiley-Interscience; 1984. Both a textbook and reference for researchers in the field.

Weber, Marvin J. *CRC Handbook of Laser Science and Technology.* Two volumes. Boca Raton: CRC Press; 1982. A handbook of critically evaluated tabular and graphical data on lasers.

Young, M. *Optics and Lasers; Including Fibers and Integrated Optics.* 2nd ed. New York: Springer-Verlag; 1984. An introduction to applied optics including lasers and other optical devices. For the engineer and applied scientist.

Some libraries may want to establish standing orders for monographic series where all or a large proportion of the issues cover laser and laser-related topics:

Advances in Laser Spectroscopy. New York: Wiley-Interscience. v.1- ; 1978- .

Laser Applications. New York: Academic. v.1- ; 1971- .

Optical Physics and Engineering. New York: Plenum. v.1- ; 1978- .

P. N. Lebedev Physics Institute Series. New York: Plenum. v.1- ; 1961- .

Springer Series in Chemical Physics. New York: Springer-Verlag. v.1- ; 1978- .

Springer Series in Optical Sciences. New York: Springer-Verlag. v.1- ; 1976- .

Topics in Applied Physics. New York: Springer-Verlag. v.1- ; 1973- .

Wiley Series in Pure and Applied Optics. New York: Wiley-Interscience.

Conferences, Proceedings, Government Reports, Patents

Conference proceedings constitute a significant portion of the early reports on laser advances. The majority of conferences in the field are published and sponsored by societies as part of a broader meeting program:

AIP Conference Series. New York: American Institute of Physics. v.1- ; 1970- .

IEEE Conference on Lasers and Electro-optics. New York: Institute of Electrical and Electronics Engineers. v.1- ; 1981- .

Institute of Physics Conference Series. Bristol. v.1- ; 1967- .

International Congress of Applications of Lasers and Electro-optics. Toledo: Laser Institute of America.

Laser Interaction and Related Plasma Phenomena; Proceedings of the Workshop held at Rensselaer Polytechnic Institute. New York: Plenum. v.1- ; 1971- .

Materials Research Society Symposia. New York: Elsevier. v.1- ; 1981- .

NATO Advanced Study Institute. Series A: Life Sciences. New York: Plenum. v.1- ; 1975- .

NATO Advanced Study Institute. Series B: Physics. New York: Plenum. v.1- ; 1974- .

NATO Advanced Study Institute. Series C: Mathematical and Physical Sciences. Dordrecht: D. Reidel. v.1- ; 1973- .

Proceedings of SPIE, the International Society for Optical Engineering. Bellingham. v.1- ; 1963- .

Topical Meeting on Integrated and Guided Wave Optics. New York: Institute of Electrical and Electronics Engineers. v.1- ; 1972- .

BIBLIOGRAPHIES

The National Technical Information Service is a ready source for recurring bibliographies on a number of laser topics.

Blood Flow Measurement: Laser Techniques 1975-January, 1985 (Citations from INSPEC). Contains 71 citations on this medical application of laser technology.

Carbon Dioxide Lasers: 1970-March, 1985 (Citations from the Engineering Index Data Base).

Laser Research. Semimonthly reports. Digests of articles from the Energy Data Base dating back to 1974.

Laser Scanning: Technology and Applications 1970-March, 1985 (Citations from the NTIS Data Base). Contains 231 citations.

Bibliography of Soviet Laser Developments. A bimonthly compilation of citations to Russian research and application.

With one exception other published bibliographies are primarily historical.

Belforte, David A.—*Industrial Laser Materials Processing Bibliography.* 3rd ed., 4 vols. Strubridge: Belfonte Associates; 1984. Section I—Laser Welding; Section II—Laser Cutting/Drilling/Machinery; Section III—Surface Treatment; Section IV—General Laser Processing.

Ionescer, Valentin—*Laser Applications in Plasma Physics (1962–1968) (Bibliography).* Vienna: International Atomic Energy Agency; 1969. A bibliography with abstracts to books, journal articles, conference proceedings and reports on plasma diagnostic and production by lasers. Includes another and KWIC indexes.

Kamal, A.—*Laser Abstracts,* vol. 1. New York: Plenum; 1964. Over 700 references with abstracts to bibliographies, books, journal and conference papers. Contains author and classified subject index. Roso, Dieter Lasers, Light Amplifiers and Oscillators. London: Academic, 1969. Includes a comprehensive bibliography of papers from scientific periodicals arranged alphabetically by author.

Tomiyaon, Kiyo—*Laser Literature: an annotated guide.* New York: Plenum; 1968. A classified arrangement under 27 categories of 3,990 references to bibliographies, books, and papers, from conferences and periodicals.

ABSTRACTING AND INDEXING SERVICES

All of the abstracting and indexing services will provide coverage of the literature in laser science and technology. Undoubtedly, indexes concentrating in applied physics will furnish more in-depth scrutiny of this precision instrument. Nevertheless, the user must be wary concerning the individual approach of each service. Including the detailed subject inclusion, list of sources, access points, types of publications included and timeliness of references. Presented here are the most relevant printed sources and a short description of their coverage. There will naturally be some overlap between the various publications.

Physics Abstracts. Science Abstracts A. London: Institution of Electrical Engineers, v.1- ; 1898- .

> The physics portion of the INSPEC Database, a service that produces abstracts of journals, conference proceedings, monographs, reports and theses published world-wide in the fields of physics, electrical engineering, electronics, computer and control. Abstracts appear semimonthly in classified arrangement. Lasers are treated principally in the OPTICS SECTION (4200) under LASERING PROCESSORS (4255) and LASER SYSTEMS AND LASER BEAM APPLICATIONS (4260). Twice yearly subject indexes provide a more analytical approach to specific topics.

Electrical and Electronics Abstracts. Science Abstracts, Series B. London: Institution of Electrical Engineers, v.1- ; 1898-

> The electrical and electronics engineering portion of the INSPEC database, which publishes abstracts on laser engineering in the OPTICAL MATERIALS AND APPLICATIONS SECTION (4000) under LASERS AND MASERS (4300). There is considerable duplication in coverage between the Physics and Electrical and Electronics sections. Indexing is identical to *Physics Abstracts*.

Engineering Index. New York: Engineering Information, Inc., v.1- ; 1884- .

> A monthly compendium of citations and abstracts to the world's literature on technological subjects. The abstracts are arranged under main subject headings and subdivisions; the main heading

appearing in alphabetical sequence. Literature sources include journal and conference papers, monographs and other materials. A printed thesaurus, *Subject Headings for Engineering,* provides controlled vocabulary subject terms. The principle terms used for identifying laser literature are LASER BEAMS; LASERS; LASERS, CARBON DIOXIDE; LASERS, CHEMICAL; LASERS, DYE; LASERS, GAS; LASERS, SEMICONDUCTOR; and LASERS, SOLID-STATE. The subdivision is used extensively under other main headings. The monthly issues cumulate in an annual set of volumes with an author index for the year. A companion publication of engineering meetings, available separately, indexes individual papers to over 2,000 conferences.

Science Citation Index. Philadelphia: Institute for Scientific Information, v.1- ; 1964- .

SCI is unique for the nature of its access to the scientific literature. Through its citation index the user may trace referees to significant papers forward in time. SCI's wide coverage of the world's literature gives the user an interdisciplinary approach not available in any other tool. Coverage includes the important journals and books in science, medicine, agriculture, technology and the behavioral sciences. Bimonthly indices for cited author, source author, and permuterm subjects are cumulated annually. Multi-year cumulations are also available.

Government Reports Announcement and Index. Springfield: National Technical Information Service, v.1- ; 1946-

A biweekly index containing summaries of United States and foreign research reports from the NTIS bibliographic data base. Abstracts are arranged under 22 broad fields with lasers entered under FIELD 20: PHYSICS; GROUP E: MASERS AND LASERS. Keyword, Contract Number, NTIS Order Number, Author and Organizational Indices are included in each issue; and subsequently cumulated and distributed hard bound at the end of the year.

Index to Scientific and Technical Proceedings. Philadelphia: Institute for Scientific Information, v.1- ; 1978- .

A monthly publication indexing selectively conferences and individual papers in all of the sciences, engineering, agriculture and medicine. The citation and contents pages are arranged in accession number order with separate general category, permuterm subject and author indexes. The monthly issues are cumulated annually with a set of bound volumes.

Other major indexes that supply references to laser applications in their particular field of coverage include *Chemical Abstracts, Index Medicus, Metals Abstracts,* and *International Aerospace Abstracts. Applied Science and Technology Index* and *General Science Index* provide broad but less than in-depth coverage of the literature, more suitable for the non-specialist.

Current Awareness

Journal of Current Laser Abstracts. Rolling Hills: Institute for Laser Documentation, v.1- ; 1964- .

> A monthly publication of abstracts covering the world's literature on laser theory and application. Abstracts are arranged under four broad categories: General Laser Publications; Theoretical Abstracts of Lasers; Experimental Laser Research and Applications of Lasers. All types of publications are scanned including patents. The publication's focus on lasers and the timely appearance of references make this an ideal tool for current awareness.

Laser-Raman & Infrared Spectroscopy Abstracts. London: PRM Science & Technology Agency, v.1- ; 1971- .

> One of a series of specialist Abstract Journals in the field of analytical techniques. This, the sixth in the series, is published bimonthly with author and subject indexes. The abstracts are arranged in accession number order under broad headings.

Current Contents. Philadelphia: Institute for Scientific Information.

> ISI publishes several weekly compilations of content pages from journals in the chemical, physical, life and engineering disciplines.

Official Gazette of the U.S. Patent and Trademark Office. Washington: v.1- ; 1872- .

> A weekly publication of U.S. patent abstracts arranged in three general categories: *General and Mechanical; Chemical; Electrical.* Lasers appear for the most part in the Electrical

section under class 372. Each patent reference includes a drawing and the first claim. Full specifications are available at public depositories in all of the major cities throughout the United States.

Weekly Abstract Newsletters. Arlington: National Technical Information Service.

NTIS makes available weekly abstract updates taken from their bibliographic data base. One may subscribe to any one of 27 categories. For the laser enthusiast the *Electrotechnology, Manufacturing Technology, Biomedical Technology, Chemistry, Communication* and *Foreign Technology* issues would be most useful.

Databases

The major vendors, *Bibliographic Retrieval Systems* (BRS), *Dialog Information Services* and the *Systems Development Corporation* (SDC) provide computer access to a number of data files containing information on laser science and technology. A search of term laser(s) in each database yielded a comparative analysis of depth in coverage. The number of citations reported is given at the end of each description.

CA SEARCH. Columbus: Chemical Abstracts Service. 1967- . Equivalent to *Chemical Abstracts.* BRS, Dialog, SDC. 88,699.

COMPENDEX. New York: Engineering Information, Inc. 1970- . Equivalent to *Engineering Index.* BRS, Dialog, SDC. 40, 301.

CONFERENCE PAPERS INDEX. Washington: Cambridge Scientific Abstracts. 1973- . Indexes some 100,000 papers from about 1,000 scientific and technical symposia. Dialog. 635 citations for 1984 only.

EI, ENGINEERING MEETINGS. New York: Engineering Information, Inc. 1982- . Indexes individual papers from about 2,000 meetings each year. Dialog, SDC. 1,766 citations for 1984 only.

MEDLINE. Bethesda: National Library of Medicine. 1966– Equivalent to *Index Medicus, Index to Dental Literature* and *International Nursing Index.* BRS, Dialog, SDC. 8,903.

INSPEC. London, England: Institution of Electrical Engineers. 1969– . Equivalent to *Physics Abstracts, Electrical and Electronics Abstracts* and *Computer and Control Abstracts*. BRS, SDC, Diaglog. 92,934.

NTIS. Springfield: National Technical Information Service. 1964– . Equivalent to *Government Reports Announcement and Index*. BRS, Dialog, SDC. 32,811.

SCISEARCH. Philadelphia: Institute for Scientific Information. 1974– . Equivalent to *Science Citation Index* and *Current Contents*. Dialog. 43,733.

ORGANIZATIONS

Societies

Broadly-based societies such as the American Institute of Physics and Institute of Electrical and Electronics Engineers in the United States and the Institute of Physics and Institute of Electrical Engineers in Great Britain actively advance laser art and science through their meetings and publications programs. Societies in other disciplines will reflect their interest to the extent that laser devices are applied to solve problems in their areas of concern. One organization has been established as a focal point for laser specialists, the Laser Institute of America (LIA). LIA was founded in 1968 and maintains its central office in Toledo, Ohio. LIA sponsors annual conferences, continuing education courses, promotes standards, bestows awards, and in other ways strives to advance laser technology. The Institute publishes a bimonthly newsletter, a safety and material processing guide and course notes.

Government Agencies and Research Laboratories

The federal government funds the bulk of laser research in the United States. There are three major sponsors: Department of Energy, Department of the Air Force and Department of the Navy. Research is conducted for the Department of Energy at the Argonne, Lawrence Livermore, Los Alamos and

Oak Ridge National Laboratories. Both the Air Force and Navy operate their own research laboratories. The National Aeronautics and Space Administration maintains its research facilities at various centers throughout the United States. The National Bureau of Standards, through its several laboratories, conducts a significant amount of laser research to further advances in physical measurement. Federal agencies not only sponsor and conduct research, but also acquire patents growing out of that effort.

Industrial Research Laboratories

About 150 industrial laboratories maintain research efforts in the field of lasers and their applications. The giant corporations that we would expect are there. Allied, Battelle, DuPont, General Dynamics, General Electric, GTE, Litton Industries, Lockheed, McDonnell, Douglas, Martin Marietta, Raytheon, RCA, Rockwell International, Sperry, TRW, United Technologies and Xerox. In addition, some twenty-eight laboratories list laser research as their main activity, indicating that lasers have come into their own as a major innovation.

Central Laser Corp.
CUI Laser Corp.
DO Industries, Inc.
General Phototonics, Inc.
Helias, Inc.
Holograf
ILC Technology
International Laser
  Systems, Inc.
Jodou Laser
KMS Fusion, Inc.
Laser Analytics, Inc.
Laser Holography
Laservation, Inc.
Lasermetrics, Inc.

Laser Nucleonics, Inc.
Laser Optic, Inc.
Ostelecon, Inc.
Phase-R Corp.
Photronics Corp.
Pulse Systems, Inc.
Quantrad Corp.
Quantronix Corp.
Quantum Technology, Inc.
Research and Laser
  Technology, Inc.
Spavor Optical Research, Inc.
Spectra-Physics, Inc.
Tachisto Laser Systems, Inc.
Terr Technology Corp.
Varo, Inc.

REFERENCES

1. Bertolotti, M. *Masers and lasers; an historical approach.* Bristol: Adam Hilger, 1983.
2. Townes, Charles H. Harnessing Light. *Science 84.* 5(9):153–155; 1984 November.
3. Christensen, C. Paul. New laser source technology. *Science.* 224(4645):117–123; 1984 April 13.
4. Zieger, H. J. *Lasers.* In: Lerner, Rita G.; Trigg, George L. *Encyclopedia of physics.* London: Addison-Wesley; 1981.
5. Klauminzer, Gary K. Twenty years of commercial lasers—a capsule history. *Laser Focus.* 20(12):54–79; 1984 December.
6. Akerley, Barbara. 1985 Laser economic review and outlook. *Laser Focus.* 21(1):75–83; 1985 January.
7. Saunders, Richard J. Laser metalworking. *Metal Progress.* 126(2):45–51; 1984 July.
8. Harvey, Robert F. Lasers: a revolutionary tool in the manufacturing environment. *Chilton's Iron Age.* 226(13):48–55; 1984 July 4.
9. Holmes, Lewis. Commercial lasers—the next five years. *Laser Focus.* 21(5):146–154; 1985 May.
10. Goldman, Leon. Laser surgery and medicine in the next decade. *Laser Focus.* 20(10):104–106; 1984 October.
11. Johnson, Roger S. Lasers invade the operating room. *High Technology.* 4(11):16–17; 1984 November.
12. Townes, Charles H. Harnessing light. *Science 84.* 5(9):153–155; 1984 November.
13. UV laser cuts cleanly. *New Scientist.* 102(1047):21; 1984 April 26.
14. Lasers could shed light on crop deficiencies: *Journal of the American Dietetic Association.* 85(3):363; 1985 March.
15. Lasers in space check on crops. *Science Digest.* 92(6):18; 1984 June.
16. Chown, Marcus. Lasers measure the Earth's movement. *New Scientist.* 105(1440):40; 1985 January 24.
17. Stepney, Rob. Holography earns its keep. *New Scientist.* 102(1409):44–56; 1984 July.
18. Robinson, Arthur L. Free electron lasers show their power. *Science.* 226(4680):1300–1302; 1984 December 14.
19. Hecht, Jeff. Opening a Pandora's box of laser weaponry. *New Scientist.* 105(1437):10–11; 1985 January 3.
20. Elson, Benjamin M. Lasers may supply space energy needs. *Aviation Week and Space Technology.* 121(12):83–89; 1984 September 17.

NEW REFERENCE WORKS IN SCIENCE AND TECHNOLOGY

Robert G. Krupp, Editor

Reviewers for this column are: Carmela Carbone (CC), Engineering Societies Library, New York, NY; Kerry Kresse (KLK), University of Kentucky, Lexington, KY; Robert G. Krupp (RGK), Maplewood, NJ; Ellis Mount (EM), Columbia University, New York, NY; and Barbara List (BL), University of Michigan, Ann Arbor, MI.

EARTH SCIENCES

Annotated bibliographies of mineral deposits in Europe. Part 1: Northern Europe including examples from the USSR in both Europe and Asia. By John Drew Ridge. New York: Pergamon Press; 1984. 778p. $120.00. ISBN 0-08-030242-4. (ISBN 0-08-024022-4 for set.)

This is another volume (in two parts) designed to discuss major ore deposits of the world for which the published literature is adequate for a study as provided by the author and compiler. All ore districts of northern Europe are included, however only a small sample of those available from the Soviet Union (mainly for language reasons) was chosen. Most of the references are in English though. Extensive author notes show (1) location of deposit, grade and tonnage of the ore (but this is not available for deposits in the Soviet Union); (2) the stratigraphy and structure of the rocks; (3) the characteristics of the ore bodies; (4) age of deposit; and (5) the reasons for the position assigned to it in the modified Lindgren classification. Countries covered are Ireland, Great Britain, Norway, Sweden, Finland, Poland, and the Soviet Union. The number of references for the geographical areas is rather small (5 to 20 for each) but carefully selected. Eleven sketched outline (but adequate) maps are included. Five indices are provided for authors and deposits. This work has been prepared to aid economic geologists. (RGK)

Index to maps in earth science publications, 1963–1983. Compiled by John Van Balen. Westport, CT: Greenwood; 1985. 400p. $49.95. ISBN 0-313-24963-6.

A cartobibliography which lists some 4,900 maps, covering 320 geographic areas published in selected earth science journals between 1981 and 1982 and in selected monographs between 1963 and 1983. Spatial coverage of individual maps varies, ranging from mineral deposits of 100 meters to those global in scope. Topics covered include coastal geomorphology, plate tectonics, mineralization zones, and location of fossil faunas. Part I lists maps geographically; Part II is a listing of sources; and Part III is an author index. (RGK)

ENGINEERING–TECHNOLOGY

Alternate energy sources VI. Four volume set. Edited by T. Nejat Veziroglu. New York: Hemisphere; 1985. 2,385p. $375.00(set). ISBN 0-89116-427-8(set). Vol. 1: Solar energy and applications, 553p. $87.00. ISBN 0-89116-428-6. Vol. 2: Solar applications/waste energy, 618p. $87.00 ISBN 0-89116-429-4. Vol. 3: Wind/ocean/nuclear/hydrogen, 613p. $87.00. ISBN 0-89116-430-8. Vol. 4: Conservation/management/policy, 601p. $87.00. ISBN 0-89116-431-6.

Though this is a series of reports on a 1983 conference and is not in a format normally designed as a ready-reference tool, it is nevertheless a most valuable compendium for reference to advances in alternative energy research and development with subject areas indicated by the titles of the four volumes. Each volume is separately and thoroughly indexed. Not only for scientists and engineers, but also for architects, planners, and other decision makers in industry and academe. (RGK)

Apple II/IIe/IIc expansion guide. By Gary Phillips and Michael Fisher. Blue Ridge Summit, PA: TAB; 1985. 307p. $22.95. ISBN 0-8306-0901-6.

A work compiled for owners of various Apple computers who want to buy expansion hardware. Provides hundreds of competitive products and reviews them in a manner which makes effective comparison shopping possible. Many photographs and a thorough index. For public libraries with serious collections on computer science. (RGK)

(The) automotive security system design handbook. By J. Daniel Gifford. Blue Ridge Summit, PA: TAB; 1985. 227p. $18.95. ISBN 0-8306-0734-X.

This is a handbook of information that can be used to protect a car (or any vehicle). The main focus is on electronic security systems. The text is written specifically for automotive and electronics hobbyists who want to design, build, and install their own system in their own vehicle. The range covered is from simple relay-type systems to a fearsome thief-stopper that rivals a computer in complexity. Rather adequately illustrated. For public libraries but best for personal purchase. (RGK)

Bowker's complete sourcebook of personal computing 1985. New York: Bowker; 1985. 1050p. $19.95. ISBN 0-8352-1931-3(pbk).

> A guide based on available information of microcomputers, and virtually any product or organization related to microcomputers including hardware, software, peripherals, magazines, user groups, books, and directories. For example, there are included 3,300 review citations for the forementioned topics, and 3,300 reviews in popular computer magazines. And in fact there are also 750 computers mentioned, 1,800 organizations, 500 in-depth profiles (machines, programs, and the like), and a listing of 545 magazines. This work is truly authoritative and a must for any library which has even just the word "computer" in its files. (RGK)

(The) Brown book: Industry guide for microcomputer pricing. Quarter 1 (1985). Oakland, CA: Adventure Capital Corporation. $250 annually. ISSN 0882-0651.

> The purpose of this new quarterly (actually an encyclopedia of popular computer prices and products) is to inform the microcomputer user industry which will in turn stabilize pricing and stimulate new product sales as well as establish benchmarks for a new aftermarket in microproducts. Coverage involves over 200 manufacturers and more than 600 individual models. For special and large public libraries. (RGK)

Buyer's guide to component TV. By Carl and Barbara Giles. Blue Ridge Summit, PA: TAB; 1985. 214p. $19.95. ISBN 0-8306-0881-8.

> The products surveyed in this reference work show in detail what is available in the area of component television for use in a household which is considering its needs for communication lifelines. Though no retail price sug-

gestions are included, the guide is a source of probably the best buys. Excellent illustrative matter. For public libraries and personal purchase. (RGK)

Compendium of safety data sheets for research and industrial chemicals. Edited by Lawrence H. Keith and Douglas B. Walters. Deerfield Beach, FL: VCH; 1985. 1862p. $270.00. ISBN 0-89573-313-7.

It is the object of this compendium to provide in a single source the most commonly sought and useful information for safety-oriented needs involving chemicals for both research and industry. It provides a guide to safe usage, storage, cleanup and shipping regulations, and personal protection. The information is compiled from over fifty reference sources. The majority of the compounds in the compendium are drawn from information provided by the National Toxicology Program. The three-volume set contains detailed information on 867 different chemicals. It is anticipated that supplemental volumes will be published. (CC)

Computer work stations. By Herman Holtz. New York: Chapman and Hall; 1985. 302p. $24.50. ISBN 0-412-00491-7.

This is not a technical treatise but is devoted to aiding the manager understand the various work station configurations possible, their differences, the criteria to be considered in analyzing needs, and then arriving at a sensible configuration to be opted for. This work will equip managers to understand the technical experts and to work with them. The reader is assumed to be a lay person in the field of computers. The author is an electronics engineer and a consultant. (RGK)

Corrosion and deposits from combustion gases. Abstracts and index. Edited by Jerrold E. Radway. New York: Hemisphere Publishing Co.; 1985. 575p. $95.00. ISBN 0-89116-301-8.

> This volume is in three sections: key words (328), abstract reproductions and reference identification, alphabetically by author (3780), and an index of abstracts arranged by most of the key words or phrases. Some of the more general terms have a great number of references, such as "coal" with 344 or "deposits" with 314. Translations of references are also noted in the second section. For engineering libraries concerned with the corrosion of steam boilers and gas-turbines, especially by combustion gases. (RGK)

Deterioration of dams and reservoirs; Examples and their analysis. Edited by the Laboratoris de Engenharia Civil, Lisbon. Rotterdam: A. A. Balkema; 1984. 367p. 118 tables. $49.50. ISBN 90-6191-546-5.

> This work is the result of twelve years of study on the deterioration of dams and reservoirs. Fourteen thousand, seven hundred dams situated in 33 countries are listed, representing 90% of the total number of dams in the world. Of these, 1105 cases of deterioration are recorded, including 107 failures. The detailed analysis of each case highlights the main causes, methods of detection, and remedial steps taken. The entire report was translated from Portuguese into English and French which are presented side by side in the textual sections and as separate headings for duplicate tables. Included is an extensive set of appendixes (about 50% of the presentation) which replicates the questionnaire itself and the answers elicited. The book is indeed an encyclopedia of case studies on dam failures. (RGK)

Encyclopedia of electronics. Edited by Stan Gibilisco. Blue Ridge Summit, PA: TPR; 1985. 983p. $60.00 ISBN 0-8306-2000-1.

> This encyclopedia is a source of information on all aspects of electricity, electronics, and communications technology. It is intended as a permanent reference source for professionals, students, and hobbyists. The more than 3000 articles are listed in alphabetical order. Related articles are listed in the text and at the end of each article. The encyclopedia has three basic parts: preceding the alphabetically arranged articles there are articles by category along with a table of schematic symbols; the largest part of the book consists of the articles themselves; a detailed index follows the articles. (CC)

Getting great graphics. By Cary N. Prague and James E. Hammitt. Blue Ridge Summit, PA: TAB; 1985. 236p. $25.95. ISBN 0-8306-0876-1.

> This work examines all the different types of graphs, the elements of graphs, and the proper techniques for creating graphics. Included too is an analysis of today's best selling graphics software packages and hardware devices. There is a strong emphasis on pictorial exhibitions. For industry, the public library, and personal purchase. (RGK)

Handbook of applied meteorology. Edited by David D. Houghton. New York: Wiley; 1985. 1461p. $84.95. ISBN 0-471-081404-2.

> This mammoth handbook presents, for the first time, an authoritative, concise, and comprehensive reference for meteorological knowledge and technology, designed for professionals and technicians *outside the meteorological profession*. This work will be an efficient reference tool for all meteorological factors that apply in a wide variety of engineering, architectural, agricultural, and aeronautical situations, to name only a few. In addition to sections on

applications, measurements, and societal impacts, the one on resources is quite in depth as to literature and its availability in research centers and libraries. A "must" acquisition for all science and technology collections in academe and industry, and, despite its cost (which is really not unreasonable for this tome), larger public libraries. (RGK)

(The) handbook of data communications and computer networks. By Dimitris N. Chorafas. Princeton: Petrocelli; 1985. 560p. $59.95. ISBN 0-89433-244-9.

This handbook is divided into areas such as the concept of distributed information systems, telecommunications, conventions governing the control of data, the generation of networks, transaction-based messages, systems induced by software, and network maintenance. It is of value to any collection dealing with data transmission systems. (RGK)

Handbook of enzyme biotechnology. 2d ed. Edited by Alan Wiseman. New York: Halstead; 1985. 457p. $82.95. ISBN 0-420-20153(sic). (The correct ISBN is 0-470-20153-3.)

This rewritten reference work takes a broad overview of enzyme biotechnology today systematically establishing the theory and practice of large-scale enzyme manufacture and utilization. Principles and practice are discussed in connection with utilization both in free and immobilized form. Very heavily documented. For biochemical collections in academe and industry. (RGK)

Handbook of industrial robotics. Edited by Shimon Y. Nof. New York: Wiley; 1985. 1358p. $62.95. ISBN 0-471-89684-5.

The growing amount of information about industrial robotics and its multidisciplinary nature have created the need for this comprehensive handbook. Its compilation was guided by the following objectives: (1) to combine up-to-date material, prepared by leading authorities, on research, development, and applications of industrial robotics; (2) to provide engineers and decision makers with an overview of industrial robotics; (3) to present techniques that are available, or will shortly be available, for practitioners in this area; (4) to provide in one volume material that can be used in courses on robotics for university and continuing education students; and (5) to motivate and encourage more investigators to become active in this field and to further advance its technical level. The book has 77 chapters containing the most current information on the research, development, design and applications of industrial robots. Each chapter includes numerous tables, formulas and photographs. Extensive bibliographies are provided. Appendices give information on international markets for industrial robots, organizations and manufacturers, and journals on the subject. A glossary of robotics terminology is also included. (CC)

Handbook of microcomputer-based instrumentation and controls. By John D. Lenk. New York: Prentice-Hall; 1984. 307p. $24.95. ISBN 0-13-380519-0.

A "crash course" reference work in digital or microcomputer-based instrumentation and control systems for engineers, technicians, programmer/analysts, and hobbyists. Technical accuracy is not sacrificed; simple, nontechnical terms are used throughout. Provides both background and a detailed look at the real world of instrumentation and control. (RGK)

Handbook of pultrusion technology. By Raymond W. Meyer. New York: Chapman and Hall; 1985. 180p. $27.50. ISBN 0-412-00761-4.

Designed to orient engineers in fundamentals concerning pultruded products and fiberglass reinforced plastic products in general. Coverage involves areas such as formulations and machines, and a collection of six vital appendixes important to this growth technology. Included is an excellent annotated bibliography with strong patent representation. For collections needing development in reinforced plastics and composites. (RGK)

How to repair and maintain your Apple computer. All II series models, including the IIc. By Gene B. Williams. Radnor, PA: Chilton; 1985 212p. $12.95. ISBN 0-8019-7549-2(pbk).

This how-to-do-it reference work shows the ease of diagnose and repair of most malfunctions of the Apple computer. A background of electronics is not necessary but helpful. Very adequately illustrated. Provides a list of the simple tools needed to do the repairs. For personal purchase and public libraries. (RGK)

ICP software directory. 7 vol. set. 54th ed. Indianapolis: ICP World Software Information Center; 1985. $745.00 (for two editions per year). ISBN 0-88094-050-6(set). Vol. 1. *Systems software,* 732p. $175.00.* ISBN 0-88094-051-4. Vol. 2. *General accounting systems,* 386p. $125.00.* ISBN 0-88094-052-2. Vol. 3. *Management and administrative systems,* 334p. $125.00.* ISBN 0-88094-053-0. Vol. 4. *Banking, insurance, and finance systems,* 257p. $125.00.* ISBN 0-88094-051-4 (same as for Vol. 1. . .sic?) Vol. 5. *Manufacturing and engineering,* 345p. $125.00.* ISBN 0-88094-055-7. Vol. 6. *Specialized industry systems,* 458p. $125.00.* ISBN 0-88094-056-5. Vol. 7 (part 1). *Microcomputer systems,* 958p. $145.00.** ISBN 0-88094-057-3. Vol. 7 (part 2). *Microcomputer systems.* 856p. $145.00.** ISBN 0-88094-058-1.

This massive, multivolume set contains application- or industry-targeted software product and service descriptions. The first six volumes deal with large-, medium-

---

*for two editions per year.
**the price for both parts 1 and 2 together.

scale, and minicomputers for general applications or for specific industries. The seventh volume, consisting exclusively of microcomputer software, is in two parts: one features systems software and general business applications, and two gives descriptions for specialized applications. For business and industrial computer service libraries. (RGK)

(The) illustrated buyer's guide to used airplanes. By Bill Clark. Blue Ridge Summit, PA: TAB; 1985. 279p. $15.95. ISBN 0-8306-2372-8(pbk).

This guide will help in economical-decision-making and allow avoidance of pitfalls found in aircraft purchasing and ownership. Includes descriptions of some 200 airplanes (usually with a photograph) commonly found as used machines. Specifications are included. There is a price guide based on the "current market". For personal purchase and public libraries. (RGK)

(The) illustrated dictionary of electronics. 3d ed. By Rufus P. Turner and Stan Gibilisco. Blue Ridge Summit, PA: TAB; 1985. 595p. $34.95. ISBN 0-8306-0866-4.

A rather standard but necessary dictionary of some 25,000 electronic terms and about 700 diagrams to supplement them. For most special and public libraries. (RGK)

Illustrated dictionary of microelectronics and microcomputers. Compiled by R. C. Holland. New York: Pergamon; 1985. 162p. $30.00 ISBN 0-08-031634-4.

The introduction of new electronic devices and systems, particularly the microcomputer, has been so rapid that a large number of new expressions have come into common use by workers in the field. This book is an attempt to present a coherent explanation of this new technology. All recent circuits, systems and applications are described. Some 9,000 terms are presented alphabetically and (about 300) illustrations are included when a diagrammatic approach assists the definitions. In this way the book is more than a glossary of terms; it presents detailed explanations of this new technology. Although aimed primarily at the electronics engineer and student, the book should be a useful reference work for the computer science student, computer hobbyist, and business computer user. (CC/RGK)

Instrument engineers' handbook: process control. Rev. ed. Edited by Béla G. Lipsták. Radnor, PA: Chilton; 1985. 1110p. $75.00. ISBN 0-8019-7290-6.

This volume on process control emphasizes elements of the control loop such as transmitters, telemetering systems and data highways, logic devices, regulators and safety valves, and the like. In addition to hardware there are included specific control systems for equipment such as boilers, compressors, and heat exchangers. The other volume, on process *measurement,* is meant to complement this one. For all collections intended to satisfy the needs of instrument engineers. The index is most extensive. (RGK)

Leading consultants in technology. 2d ed. Woodbridge, CT: Research Publications; 1985. (Dist. by Gale) 2 vols. $195.00/set. ISBN 0-89235-089-X.

Lists 18,000 consultants who are specialists in technical subjects. The persons described were selected from *Who's Who in Technology Today,* a comprehensive biographical reference source. Volume 1 lists the consultants' biographical sketches, arranged by disciplines and sub-disciplines (such as Electronics sub-divided into electronics, computer science, control systems, etc.) Contains pure sciences as well as engineering/technology. Volume 2 contains a list by specific types of expertise or skills, along with an alphabetical index of consultants' names. Typical terms in the expertise index include laser, latex, lattice, lead, lens, light, etc. Should prove to be a useful index in any sci-tech library in locating individuals with special skills. (EM)

Manufacturing processes and materials for engineers. By Lawrence E. Doyle. 3d ed. Englewood Clliffs, NJ: Prentice-Hall; 1985. ISBN 0-13-555921-9.

This book covers major metal and plastic fabrication processes and explains them in terms of the basic engineering sciences. The book emphasizes the economic relationships that must be applied to select optimum processes. This edition adopts the SI system of dimensioning. It gives special attention to the environment, energy conservation and safety considerations. Included are the latest systems for industrial processing such as automation, flexible manufacturing systems, programmable controllers, CAD/CAM, numerical control and its programming. The book provides up-to-date information on new processes, new tools, materials, and abrasives. (CC)

McGraw-Hill personal computer programming encyclopedia: languages and operating systems. Edited by William J. Birnes. New York: McGraw-Hill; 1985. 696p. $80.00. ISBN 0-07-005389-8.

This resource examines the personal computing environment, both as a science and as a commercial industry. It presents functional and operating definitions of all the statements, commands, and source codes in 19 different programming languages. Indicates strengths and weaknesses of each language application and provides translation tables between languages and language dialects. This is a highly practical reference tool for anyone interested in personal computers and should be not only in academe but also in larger public libraries. (RGK)

Mechanical components handbook. Edited by Robert O. Parmley. New York: McGraw-Hill; 1985. Mixed pagination. $57.50. ISBN 0-07-048514-3.

> This handbook is a companion to the *Standard handbook of fastening and joining* and categorizes basic mechanical components used in current mechanical technology, and thus opens the gateway to new designs. Suitably illustrated with diagrams and photographs. For all engineering collections in academe and industry. (RGK)

Mechanical engineering for professional engineers' examination. 4th ed. By John D. Constance. New York: McGraw-Hill; 1985. 595p. $34.95. ISBN 0-07-012452-3.

> The purpose of this work is to provide the needed encouragement for practicing mechanical engineers to take the professional engineering examination and to implement the impulse and urge for them to become licensed. This edition has been revised to reflect the NCEE examination trend. Included are hundreds of problems and the detailed answers presented in a manner and format consistent with the requirements of such an examination. There is a very handy problem index. For personal purchase, public libraries, and engineering collections. (RGK)

Mines and mining equipment and service companies worldwide. 2d ed. Edited by Don Nelson. New York: Spon; 1985. 681p. $79.95. ISBN 0-419-13260-0.

> This annual (for 1985) covers aspects of the mining industry, including the principal operating and financial mining companies, and the equipment, service and consultancy companies. The main reference section (3518 entries) presents the companies in alphabetical order. There is also a geographical index and a two-part company index, first for mining companies, and second for others such as equipment manufacturers. A personnel

index refers back to the principal index as do all subsidiary indexes. For mining engineering collections. (RGK)

1985–86 encyclopedia of information systems and services. 6th ed. (two volumes). Edited by John Schmittroth, Jr. Detroit: Gale Research; 1985. Vol. 1: International volume. 669p. $190.00. ISBN 0-8103-1538-6. Vol. 2: United States volume. 1200p. $200.00. ISBN 0-8103-1541-6. For the set: ISBN 0-8103-1537-8.

This review concerns only the *International Volume* which covers more than 1,000 international and national information organizations and services located in some 65 countries but excluding the United States. Four categories of information systems are given: information providers, information access services, information industry, and support services. Entries have been expanded to include, for example, codes through which an organization can be contacted on public electronic mail networks. For all academic, public, and special library collections. (RGK)

Planning; the architect's handbook. 10th ed. Edited by Edward D. Mills. London: Butterworths; 1985. 658p. $99.95. ISBN 0-408-01213-7.

The edition celebrates the 50th year of the existence of *Planning* and is now presented in one volume (as opposed to a series of separate volumes for earlier editions). Essentially this key reference work provides basic data and information (with drawings) that are essential material before the planning of any building can commence. For the most part the work does not deal with the criteria for aesthetic or architectural solutions to design problems. Of course the work is geared to situations and conventions in the United Kingdom, but that does not prevent it from being a most useful tool elsewhere in the world where architectural design is under consideration. (RGK)

Plastics product design engineering handbook. 2d ed. By Sidney Levy and J. Harry Dubois. New York: Chapman and Hall; 1984. 360p. $22.50. ISBN 0-412-00521-2(pbk).

>This new edition has been expanded to include topics related to computer usage in the design of plastics products. Finite element analysis is introduced as a tool to evaluate structures made of plastics. Otherwise, this reference edition continues to treat the problems of the plastics product designer. Well-illustrated. For engineering design reference shelves in academe and special libraries. (RGK)

Process instruments and controls handbook. 3d ed. Edited by Douglas M. Considine. New York: McGraw-Hill; 1985. Mixed pagination. $89.50. ISBN 0-07-012436-1.

>This new edition (since 1974) is very highly revised (80% new information) and includes 1565 illustrations and 177 tables. In order to hone the work carefully due to space considerations, some 30 topics (e.g., bimetal thermometers and pressure regulators) are not included and must be referenced in the Second Edition. Deleted too are four special papers (e.g., computer-aided manufacturing/robotics, for discrete-piece handling industries) for the same reason. Despite all these exceptions and omissions, the work provides 83 articles of great length and in unbelievable detail with references for each appropriately updated. The subject index is thorough and comprehensive. For all engineering and technology collections. (RGK)

Quick reference manual for silicon integrated circuit technology. Edited by W. E. Beadle and others. New York: Wiley-Interscience; 1985. Mixed pagination. $65.00. ISBN 0-471-81588-8.

>In the semiconductor industry, extensive use is made of handy curves and graphs in design work. These aids often represent data accumulated over several years of experience by individuals or groups. Often it takes the form of a set of curves or a handy nomograph. Despite

the usefulness of such information, it usually has very limited circulation throughout the design community. This manual is a collection of such reference data gleaned by the authors in their work in the design, development, processing, manufacture, and characterization of silicon devices and integrated circuits. Included are properties of silicon, mathematical expressions, measurements, chemical recipes, diffusion, ion implantation, process data, conductivity of diffused layers, properties of p-n and metal-semiconductor junctions, MOS, and reliability. A comprehensive table of physical constants is also provided. (CC)

Reference manual for telecommunications engineering. By Roger L. Freeman. New York: Wiley-Interscience; 1985. 1504p. $75.00. ISBN 0-471-86753-5.

This is a compilation of reference information for telecommunication systems engineers. It consists of tables, graphs, figures, nomograms, formulas, and statistics that busy engineers can consult for the various kinds of data necessary in their day-to-day work. The material has been selected from a large body of papers, handbooks, monographs, standards and other sources. The aim of the book is to provide a central source of basic information that will have repeated application. It covers the basic disciplines of telecommunications, namely, transmission and switching. It also covers a number of the principal support areas such as reliability, EMI, and engineering economy. The material is subdivided into 26 subject areas with which the broadly based communication system engineer should be familiar. Each section begins with an introduction and a table of contents and ends with references and, in most cases, a bibliography. A detailed subject index is provided. (CC)

Security for you & your home: a complete handbook. By Clarence M. Kelley and Carl A. Roper. Blue Ridge Summit, PA: TAB; 1984. 391p. $29.95. ISBN 0-8306-0680-7.

> This tool provides detailed information and techniques to dramatically increase security of a variety of properties. The products cited are selected because (according to the authors) they work. Coverage involves topics such as the home, vehicles, travel, insurance, and self-protection. Included too are a variety of security checklists. Heavily illustrated. For public libraries. (RGK)

(The) Software encyclopedia, 1985/86. [Volumes 1 and 2.] New York: R. R. Bowker; 1985. 2084p. $95.00(set). ISBN 0-8352-2155-5(set).

> Provides a listing of 22,000 available software programs and packages from some 3,000 publishers. In the first volume there are four indexes: guide to applications (830 headings), applications index (somewhat lean; release dates mostly missing), title index, and publishers' index. In the second volume there is an expanded application index which is actually a repeat of the sketchy data provided under the original applications index plus other details. The compilation is of course very important and quite extensive but is in an arrangement which is rather confusing bibliographically. Nevertheless the work can serve industry and academe quite adequately and at a reasonable price. (RGK)

Standard handbook of engineering calculations. 2d ed. Edited by Tyler G. Hicks. New York: McGraw-Hill; 1985. Mixed pagination. $59.50. ISBN 0-07-028735-X.

> Provides specific engineering calculation procedures for solving routine and nonroutine problems found in twelve engineering fields such as aeronautical, civil, marine, nuclear, and sanitary. Coverage involves activities of design, operation, analysis, and economic evaluation. For

all engineering collections in industry, academe, and the larger public libraries. (RGK)

Using Framework: a pictorial guide. By Cary N. Prague and Lawrence Kasevich. Blue Ridge Summit, PA: TAB; 1985. 311p. $26.95. ISBN 0-8306-0966-0.

Framework is a new generation of integrated software which combines word processing, spreadsheets, databases, graphics, and communications. This book was produced using Framework and provides tips and explanations needed to master Framework, from windowing to programming with the Framework programming language, FRED. For those processing numbers, data, and graphs, whether a novice or an advanced user. (RGK)

Welding handbook. 7th ed. Five volume set. Miami, FL: American Welding Society. $200 (set). Vol. 1: *Fundamentals of welding,* Edited by Charlotte Weisman. 1976, rev. 1981. 373p. ISBN 0-87171-126-5. Vol. 2: *Welding processes,* Edited by W.H. Kearns. 1978. 592p. ISBN 0-87171-148-6. Vol. 3: *Welding Processes,* Edited by W. H. Kearns. 1980. 459p. IBSN 0-87171-188-5. Vol. 4: *Metals and their weldability,* Edited by W. H. Kearns. 1982. 582p. ISBN 0-87171-218-0. Vol. 5: *Engineering costs, quality, and safety,* Edited by W. H. Kearns. 1984. 444p. ISBN 0-87171-239-3.

This is a set of five volumes dealing with the many aspects of welding. It should be noted though that the copyright dates of the volumes vary from 1976 (but revised in 1981) to 1978, 1980, 1982, and 1984, hence there is represented a rather broad spread of dated material which may or may not relate appropriately from volume to volume or indeed from edition to edition. Volume 1 concerns itself only with the basic technology of welding (i.e., physics of welding, heat flow, and welding metallurgy). The data provided were chosen so that they will not become outdated before the 8th edition, due about 1990. Volume 2 covers arc and gas welding and cutting, brazing, and soldering while volume 3 continues process coverage with resistance welding, thermal spraying, and adhesive bonding. Volume 4 updates and expands information on the weldability, brazeability, and solderability of metals and their alloys. The final volume (5) has revisions of symbols for welding, brazing, nondestructive testing, and the like. Included too is new material on areas such as design for welding, fixtures, and positioners, and weld quality. The entire set now pretty much replaces the 6th edition. Preceding each volume's subject index there is an index to major subjects with respect to the 6th edition for a few topics not covered in the 7th edition. A summarization of these indexes is in Volume 5. There is no subject index *per se* for the set as a whole. For most mechanical and metallurgical engineering libraries, with a word of caution that the 6th edition (if on hand) must be retained for the sake of subject completeness. (RGK)

Wind energy technical information guide, March 1985. Golden, CO: Solar Energy Research Institute; 1985. 101p. Price not given. SERI/SP-271-2684. (A Government Depository publication.)

Written for a broad technical audience, this guide will help in the search of information in the wind energy field ranging from its history and technology to the latest in research and development. Chapter 7 on current research centers and 8 on information sources and design tools have been most carefully researched and together provide an unusual mother lode, especially for those needing to develop contacts in the field. The index is in two parts: organizations and subjects, the latter a seemingly uneven mixture of general and highly specific topics (e.g., "wind energy resource assessment" with 22 page references, "siting" with 19, and "economics" with only one although there are separate entries for "economic assessment", "Economic Recovery Tax Act", and "financing"). (RGK)

World energy directory: a guide to organizations and research activities in non-atomic energy. 2d ed. Edited by Wendy M. Smith. London: Longmans; 1985. (Dist. by Gale) 582p. $190.00. ISBN 0-582-90026-3.

> Describes the location, features and activities of more than 2,500 organizations located in 90 locations around the world. Entries are arranged by countries, then by alphabetical order. It includes all types of energy research, such as solar, geothermal, wind, coal and petroleum products. Related areas that are listed include energy conservation, electrical distribution systems and heat transfer. Organizations covered consist of academic institutions, corporations, industrial firms, professional societies and other research groups. There are two indexes, one a title listing of organizations and the other a subject index. (EM)

World nuclear directory: a guide to organizations and research activities in atomic energy. 7th ed. Edited by C. W. J. Wilson. London: Longman; 1985. (Dist. by Gale) 387p. $180.00. ISBN 0-582-90025-5.

> Providing information about nuclear research organizations in some 70 countries, this edition presents an international directory to such agencies. It includes university departments, government agencies, research institutes, corporate units, public utilities and professional societies, all engaged in nuclear research. Besides the usual data the entries describe the scope and range of research activities, surveyed as of December 1984. There are two indexes, one for subjects and the other for titles or organizations. (EM)

LIFE SCIENCES

Atlas of plant viruses. By R. I. B. Francki and others. Boca Raton, FL: CRC Press; 1985. Vol. 1: 222p. $80.00. ISBN 0-8493-6501-5. Vol. 2: 284p. $95.00. ISBN 0-8493-6502-3.

> More than 200 electron micrographs illustrate examples from 26 major groups of viruses. Each chapter describes group members and their relationships, the virus structure and composition, and then finally the cytopathology associated with this virus. The three authors compiled the book themselves in order to maintain uniformity, but credit colleagues with their help. Many of the electron micrographs were supplied by the Commonwealth Special Research Grant (Australia) and the Italian National Research Council Plant Virus Institute. Recommended for academic and special libraries. (KLK)

CRC handbook of flowering. Abraham H. Halevy, editor. Boca Raton, FL: CRC Press; 1985-. 5 volumes. $735.00 ISBN 0-8493-3911-1 (set).

> Current information on the control and regulation of flowering is brought together in this handbook. All aspects are treated, including juvenility and maturation, flower morphology, flower induction, and morphogenesis to full bloom stage. Chapters are devoted to individual plants, and have been written by experts in the field. The actual coverage of each plant is dependent on the availability of experimental information, rather than on the importance of the plant economically. A broad range of cultivated plants is included: field crops, fruits, vegetables, ornamentals, industrial plants, and forest trees. Volume 5 is due to be published in 1986 and will cover plants not included in the present volumes. (BL)

Cacti of Texas and neighboring states: a field guide. By Del Weniger. Austin: University of Texas Press; 1984. 356p. $24.95. ISBN 0-292-71085-2. (Paperback: $14.95. ISBN 0-292-71063-1.)

All forms of cacti known to be growing in Arkansas, Louisiana, New Mexico, Oklahoma, and Texas are covered in this field guide. Cacti are listed by their scientific names, followed by all common names attributed to them, including Spanish and Indian names. The entries also include descriptions, ranges of distribution, discussion of unusual or interesting features, and a color photograph of a flowering specimen. The author does point out that the photographs were not taken in the native habitat. A glossary, index of scientific names, and index of common names are found at the back of the volume. For historical and taxonomic information, readers are referred to the author's earlier book, *Cacti of the Southwest* (1970). (BL)

Cambridge encyclopedia of life sciences. Edited by Adrian Friday and David S. Ingram. Cambridge: Cambridge University Press; 1985. 432p. $39.50. ISBN 0-521-25696-8.

Although encyclopedic in nature, this new offering from Cambridge University Press tries to be something different, and succeeds admirably. The entries follow not an alphabetical arrangement, but rather a biological one. Beginning with the cell and following its development into an organism, the first section deals with processes and organization. The second section discusses the various environments (e.g., marine) and their biological and geological parts. The final section details evolution and what we can (and have) learned from the fossil record. Each section provides a nice bibliography for further reading. Very well indexed and handsomely illustrated, this book is highly recommended for all academic libraries and medium to large public libraries. Its modest price will also make it attractive for personal collections. (KLK)

(The) cyclostomata—an annotated bibliography, supplement 1979-1983. By P.J. Healey and F.W.H. Beamish. Ann Arbor, MI: Great Lakes Fishery Commission; 1984. 320p. No charge.

This volume is the second supplement to a bibliography of the same title published in 1973. The first supplement covered the years 1973–1978. The present volume contains 1332 references, most of which have been published since 1978. New references have been identified using the CAN/SDI search system which is associated with the Canada Institute for Scientific and Technical Information, National Research council of Canada. Other sources include author and government contribution. The references are arranged alphabetically by first author. There are "see also" references leading from secondary to primary author. The subject index provides access with a specified list of search words. These terms are enriched with significant words from the author's title. The list of search words includes geographical locations, fossil names, general taxonomic names, species names and biological terms. (BL)

(A) dictionary of birds. Edited by Bruce Campbell and Elizabeth Lack. Published for the British Ornithologists' Union. Vermillion, SD: Buteo Books; 1985. 670p. $75.00. ISBN 0-931130-12-3.

This volume is an extensively revised update of Landsborough Thomson's *A New Dictionary of Birds* (1964). The new material reflects the rapidly expanding field of ornithology and hence makes this work a valuable resource for both public libraries and specialized science libraries. Approximately 280 experts have contributed articles on general subjects relating to birds, and on different kinds of birds approached at the family level. Many of the articles are quite long, giving this dictionary the quality of an encyclopedia. A good number of the articles are supplemented with a list of references to mainly English language literature. There are nearly 500 photographs depicting bird activities such as courtship, and some 200 drawings. The editors point out that this volume does not cover terms that can be found in "ordinary" dictionaries. (BL)

(A) dictionary of genetics. 3d ed. By Robert C. King and William D. Stansfield. New York: Oxford University Press; 1985. 480p. $35.00. ISBN 0-19-503494-5. (Paperback: $16.95. ISBN 0-19-503495-3.)

This edition has grown by over 2000 entries since the 2nd edition appeared in 1972. Its development is a reflection of both the tremendous expansion of knowledge in the field of genetics and the broad, interdisciplinary nature of the discipline. The editors have attempted to compile a dictionary that will serve the specialist and the nonspecialist alike. To aid the novice, for example, common acronyms have been identified and defined. Also, commonly studied species and genera are described in terms of their usefulness to geneticists. One appendix gives a classification of living organisms, while another lists scientific names of common domesticated species. Another helpful feature is the chronology of important events beginning with the invention of the compound microscope in 1590 and ending with the Nobel Prize laureates of 1984. The chronology is complemented by a bibliography of major sources that went into its development. Finally, there is a list of 393 periodicals cited in the literature of genetics, cytology, and molecular biology. The definitions themselves are concise and to the point. (BL/KLK)

Directory of North American fisheries scientists. Mary J. Lewis, editor. Baltimore, MD: American Fisheries Society; 1984. 398p. $30.00. ISBN 0-913235-18-0.

This is the first edition of the *Directory,* and it provides information on 8,178 aquatic or fisheries scientists. The data compiled were taken from a questionnaire sent out to academic institutions, government agencies, industry, and professional societies. Section 1 is an alphabetical listing of individuals, and includes degrees, title, addresses, telephone numbers, and subject specialty. Individuals are grouped by their areas of expertise in the second section, and by geographic area in the third. (BL)

(A) field guide to southern mushrooms. By Nancy Smith Weber and Alexander H. Smith. Ann Arbor: The University of Michigan Press; 1985. 280p. Paperback: $16.50. ISBN 0-472-85615-4.

The authors are old hands at producing mushroom field guides and do so with great expertise. In this volume they have concentrated on mushrooms that grow in the Appalachian highlands, the Mississippi Delta, and the coastal plains along the Gulf of Mexico and the Atlantic Ocean. Of the 3,000 to 5,000 mushrooms thought to occur in the South, 241 species appear in this guide. Species included fit at least one of the following criteria: they are good to eat, are common and conspicuous, or are poisonous; they illustrate the diversity of fungi; are special challenges to collectors; or are of special interest in some other way. All species are illustrated with color photographs, most often in their natural habitat. Species descriptions cover important identification characteristics, data on microscopic features, edibility, when and where to find the mushroom, and various observations that will be of interest to the collector. In the appendices a beginner can find a list of edible species recommended for the neophyte, a glossary, a bibliography, and an index, along with other useful lists. (BL)

Forestry and forestry products vocabulary. By Mirja Ruokonen. Slough, England: Commonwealth Agricultural Bureaux; 1984. 459p. $45.00. ISBN 0-85198-548-3.

This is a compilation of technical terms of forestry, forest products and related subjects that are in current use. It is not meant to be a thesaurus or prescriptive list, although it may be used as a guide when preparing house style spelling rules. It can be used as a supplement to the list of terms provided annually in *Forestry Abstracts* and *Forest Products Abstracts* and would be an aid to online database searchers as such. Both British and American spellings are given. For each concept a source from which it was taken is indicated. (BL)

(The) literature of the life sciences. By David A. Kronick. Philadelphia: ISI Press; 1985. 219p. $29.95. ISBN 0-89495-045-2.

A sound understanding of the literature is essential in order to do effective research in any field. Not only does one need to know what types of resources exist, but also why they exist and the information that they contain. Kronick, Director of the University of Texas Health Science Center at San Antonio Library from 1965 to 1984, provides an overview of the life sciences literature. He discusses, in general terms, primary and secondary sources and history and characteristics of the literature. Searching techniques, for both online and paper copy, are highlighted, as well as writing and publishing. This guide ends with an overview of personal information files and conjecture about the future. What Kronick doesn't do is to specify titles or describe specific subjects. His valid point is that enough of those monographs already exist. An interesting note: Out of the 484 item bibliography, Eugene Garfield is the most heavily cited author, with 27 items. Recommended reading for libraries, scientists and students. Recommended for purchase by life science and library science collections. (KLK)

(The) Macmillan guide to Britain's nature reserves. By Jeremy Hywel-Davies and Valerie Thom. London: Macmillan; 1984. 717p. $38.00. ISBN 0-333-35398-6.

Nearly 2,000 nature reserves in England, Wales and Scotland are documented in this lavishly illustrated guide. Arranged by region (generally counties), each is accompanied by a map and a brief introduction written by a naturalist familiar with the general area. Each reserve is described in terms of area, owner or manager, site description, restrictions and the best time to visit. It is extensively indexed by site and species (plant and animal), and also includes a glossary. Credit for publication has been given to the Royal Society for Nature Conservation and Gulf Oil Corporation. His Royal Highness the Prince of Wales contributed the forward. Recommended for nature and conservation collections in most libraries, also for personal use by experts and nature enthusiasts. (KLK)

Plants for human consumption: an annotated checklist of the edible phanerogams and ferns. Compiled by G. Kunkel. Keonigstein, FRG: Koeltz Scientific Books; 1984. 393p. $34.65. ISBN 3-87429-216-9.

The compiler has produced a checklist that combines older, standard works with recent or revised references that focus on edible plants. Considered out of scope are plants used for alcoholic beverages or smoking. Approximately 12,650 species from over 3,100 genera and 400 families are treated. The main text is organized alphabetically by genus-species. Most entries consist of very brief notes describing geographic locale, edible plant parts, and manner of consumption. The compiler makes note of the fact that an exhaustive work was not possible—such information as common names and synonyms is not included. A list of the 41 main references precedes the main body of material. In addition, the higher taxa and their families have been grouped together in one section, allowing for convenient reference. (BL)

Plants that merit attention. Volume I—Trees. The Garden Club of America. Janet Meakin Poor, editor. Portland, OR: Timber Press; 1984. lv. $44.95. ISBN 0-917304-75-6.

Trees that merit attention, according to this volume, are those that are seldom seen in our usual landscapes, are attractive additions to gardens, parks, and cityscapes, exhibit blossoms, fruits, color or interesting bark, and are tolerant to various environmental stresses. Trees are arranged alphabetically by scientific name. One page is devoted to describing each tree: its source, physical characteristics, conditions for cultivation, and landscape value. There is also a list of gardens given where a specimen can be seen. Three color photographs highlighting different features of each tree appear on the page opposite the description. In the appendices one finds a list of aboreta, botanical gardens, gardens, and parks, along with their addresses and directors' names; a directory of nursery sources; and a list of trees sorted by site and habitat characteristics. (BL)

(The) wines of America. 3d ed. By Leon D. Adams. New York: McGraw-Hill; 1985. 608p. $22.95 ISBN 0-07-00319-X.

Adams takes the reader on a leisurely and readable tour of wines in America. After a brief history, he begins a state by state description of wines and winemaking, and then journeys into Canada and Mexico. More than a third of the book is devoted to California. Adams' narrative style is quite charming, bringing out the local flavor and personalities of each area he describes. A third edition published only seven years after the second may seem surprising until you consider the creation of 450 new wineries since 1978, and the growing popularity (and respect for) domestic wines both here and abroad. It is well-indexed but sparsely illustrated. Highly recommended for all libraries, academic and public, and also for wine-lovers everywhere. (KLK)

PHYSICAL SCIENCES

Astronomical objects for southern telescopes with an addendum for northern observatories: A handbook for amateur observers. By E. J. Hartung. New York: Cambridge University Press; 1968 (first pbk. edition, 1984). 237p. $17.95. ISBN 0-521-31887-4.

> This 1984 paperback of the 1968 original is designed mainly for amateur observers of the southern sky (50° N declination and the south pole) who are not well served by existing publications. Includes an observing list of some 1,000 objects along with descriptions. For more northern observers, the remainder (12%) has been covered by an addendum. There is also a 16-page section of plates. For personal purchase certainly, but also for public libraries and observatories which do not have the original volume. (RGK)

(The) astronomical scrapbook: skywatchers, pioneers, and seekers in astronomy. By Joseph Ashbrook. New York: Cambridge University Press and Cambridge, MA: Sky Publishing Corporation; 1984 468p. $19.95. ISBN 0-521-30045-2(CUP); 0-933346-24-7(SPC).

> An anthology of articles reprinted from *Sky and Telescope* covering little known asides to the history of astronomy over a 26-year period. The compiler ferreted out these astronomical curiosities from among the crumbling and forgotten literature at the Harvard Observatory library. He also had a fondness for misfits, ill-conceived projects, and far-away places—preoccupations which happily punctuate this collection. Includes some beautiful photographs. A wonderful reference work for any front shelves in public and academic libraries (even if they are subscribers to *Sky and Telescope*) and certainly for purchase at a not outlandish price. (RGK)

Catalogue of meteorites. 4th ed., rev. and enlarged. By A. L. Graham and others. Tucson, AZ: University of Arizona Press; 1985. 460p. $50.00. ISBN 0-8165-0912-3.

> Incorporates and expands the information published in the 1966 third edition and its 1977 appendix, and includes the names of all well-authenticated meteorites known up to January 1984. There is no text except an account of the nomenclature and classification of meteorites and the system of entries. 2784 meteorites are listed and divided into 99 countries by "falls, finds, doubtful" and if located (physically) in the British Museum. For mineralogy and astronomy collections in academe, large public libraries, and observatories. (RGK)

Chemical research faculties: an international directory. Gisella Linder Pollock, Project editor. Washington, DC: American Chemical Society; 1984. 407p. $129.95. ISBN 0-8412-0817-4.

> This directory is international in scope in that it contains information on institutions in 62 countries except the United States and Canada. (These two countries are covered in the *ACS directory of graduate research 1983*.) This work is meant to provide data to facilitate the location of a colleague by chemical specialty, country, academic institution, or by name. There is a faculty index and one of research subjects. Data are given for 727 departments and some 8900 individual faculty members. For all serious chemistry collections in academic, industrial, and the larger public libraries. (RGK)

Chemistry definitions, notions, terminology. By A. I. Busev and I. P. Efimov. Translation from the Russian by V. A. Sipachev. Moscow: MIR; 1984. 295p. $7.95. (ISBN not given.)

> A collection of terms (originally intended in 1981 for Russian secondary school students) covering most aspects of chemistry and chemical engineering. There are

some 1600 entries, many with quite detailed definitions and discussions. In the appendix are a history of the discovery of the elements, industrial minerals, and SI unit definitions, all in tabular form. For chemistry collections espousing an international sense. (RGK)

Comet Halley: once in a lifetime. By Mark Littman and Donald K. Yeomans. Washington, DC: American Chemical Society; 1985. 175p. $19.95. ISBN 0-8412-0905-7.

This review is being written on the very day that the International Cometary Explorer (ICE) flew through the tail of Comet Giacobini-Zinner, the first spacecraft to fly close to and through the tail of a comet, about 5000 miles from the nucleus! Although the International Halley Watch began in 1980 (and "Halley" is pronounced to rhyme with "alley" and "O'Malley" but never with "hail"), this "fly-through" has given astronomers their first inkling of the actual make-up of a comet and thus paves the way for observations during passage of Comet Halley at 57.6 million miles from Earth on November 27, 1985 (and its return repass next Spring). All this fascinating information is elaborated on in virtual mouth-watering detail in this volume, not so much for the astronomer or scientist, but primarily for the ordinary layman who has awaited this apparition for 76 years. The text is wonderfully written, entertaining and instructional, and very heavily illustrated. In fact there are two texts: the story of comets from beginning to end and separate vignettes of one or two pages each (on brown paper) interspersed through the text proper. It is through these asides that we learn about Halley the man, superstitions regarding comets, the cometary nucleus, dust, and ion tails, explosions, the cooperation around the world in effect now, and pages of data on the "comet hall of fame," and on almost limitlessly! What a digestible fountain of information on a popular subject all rotating about this once in our lifetime encounter with the Comet Halley. This unique reference tool is for public and academic libraries of course, but what a wonderful gift to one's self! The authors are with NASA and the Jet Propulsion Laboratory, respectively. (RGK)

Electrochemical synthesis of inorganic compounds: a bibliography. By Zoltán Nagy. New York: Plenum; 1985. 474p. $75.00 ISBN 0-306-419-38-6.

This bibliography covers the 75 years ending with 1983, although a few references outside this time period are included. All original publications cited deal with the synthesis of inorganic compounds by electrochemical means (laboratory scale, and pilot and full-scale production). A few large scale processes already in operation are omitted (e.g., production of hydroxides). Each of the 76 chapters is arranged by element (alphabetical by chemical symbol) with the references in alphabetical order according to the chemical formula of the final product. A compilation not only for inorganic chemistry collections but also for those which strive to be comprehensive. (RGK)

Handbook of applicable mathematics. Volume VI: Statistics. Parts A and B. Edited by Emlyn Lloyd. New York: Wiley; 1984. 942p. plus mixed pagination for appendixes. $170.00 (set). ISBN 0-471-90024-9(set). Part A: $85.00. ISBN 0-471-90274-8; Part B: $85.00. ISBN 0-471-90272-1.

This set is as a whole a core volume (the final one) and is devoted solely to statistics. Essentially a mathematical work, it is designed specifically for the needs of the professional adult and should be considered truly a handbook (as titled) and not an encyclopedia. As such it has been written as a contribution to the practice of mathematics, not to the theory. Certainly for all serious collections on mathematics but important too for most science collections in industry and academe. (RGK)

Metals handbook. 9th ed. *Vol. 8: Mechanical testing*. Coordinated by John R. Newby. Metals Park, OH: American Society of Metals; 1985. 778p. $85.00. ISBN 0-87170-007-7(v.1).

> Although the 1948 and 1985 single-volume editions of *Metals Handbook* each include a section on mechanical testing, and Volumes 10 and 11 of the 8th edition series touch on various aspects of the subject, this marks the first time an entire Handbook volume has been devoted exclusively to this technology. Extensive attention is given tension testing. Emphasis is on metals (but does not preclude plastics). The work is designed to assist in the performance of mechanical tests and in selecting the most cost-efficient equipment to obtain valid results. Also given are descriptions of procedures and interpretation of results, all supported with in-depth literature references. The subject index is uncommonly thorough. For comprehensive physical sciences collections. (RGK)

Nuclear fact book. 2d ed. Compiled by A. M. Platt and others. New York: Harwood Academic Publishers; 1985. 176p. $33.00. ISBN 3-7186-0273-3.

> This manual is a handy reference for areas such as energy production, consumption and costs; nuclear energy production, fuel cycle, and wastes; and related fuel-cycle information. Presentations are simple and sources clearly stated. This volume first appeared as Vol. 5 Nos. 2–3 of *Radioactive waste management and the nuclear fuel cycle*. For all libraries which, even in some small way, may have to deal with nuclear power. (RGK)

Oils, lubricants, and petroleum products: characterization by infrared spectra. Compiled by John P. Coates and Lynn C. Setti. New York: Dekker; 1985. 294p. $145.00. ISBN 0-8247-7412-4.

> In an attempt to correct current deficiencies (the former use of linear wavelength presentations), this collection presents 531 spectra from a broad base of materials from

the petroleum industry (i.e., raw materials to final products), although it is not an exhaustive collection. The spectra are replots on conventional gridded chart paper and are arranged in sections that reflect their application. The volume is thus not only a reference source but also a means of identification by direct comparison of spectral data. For all analytical chemistry collections in petroleum industry infrared laboratory libraries. (RGK)

Physical properties of amorphous materials. Edited by David Adler and others. New York: Plenum; 1985. 443p. $62.50. ISBN 0-306-41907-6.

A collection of fourteen 1982–3 lectures on the fundamentals of amorphous materials and devices which at once became a reference tool of the first order on the physical properties of such solids. Though the format is not that of the usual handbook, the data embedded in the text should not be overlooked as part of the reference collections in the physical sciences. The detailed subject index is one of the keys to this work's value. (RGK)

Research in technical communication: A bibliographic sourcebook. Edited by Michael G. Moran and Debra Journet. Westport, CT: Greenwood; 1985. 515p. $57.50. ISBN 0-313-23431-0.

A reference collection of past research in technical communication for those who want to develop its future. Provides documentation of the diverse approaches this research has taken and suggests to researchers and teachers directions that seem most profitable and necessary for future work. A mother lode of information is made available in this volume on technical and scientific communication. (RGK)

SCIENCE, GENERAL

(The) Concise dictionary of science. Edited by Robin Kerrod. New York: Arco; 1985. 253p. $11.95. ISBN 0-668-06514-1.

A small but handy dictionary covering all aspects of science and technology. Has some 3,000 entries, which vary in length from a few words to half a column. Copiously illustrated on virtually every page, mostly with colored drawings or tables/charts. For the price this would be useful for lay readers to purchase or for library use. A very attractive book. (EM)

Concise encyclopaedia of information technology. 2d. ed. By Adrian V. Stokes. Brookfield, VT: Gower; 1985. 279p. $39.95. ISBN 0-566-02531-0.

Though called an "encyclopaedia" this compilation is more a dictionary in form. It defines about 3,000 computer terms, both formal and informal, with some, such as "self-modifying program", "Huffman code", and "file identifier", discussed at length. There is an appendix of over 700 acronyms and abbreviations. The work is an updated edition from 1982 but the introduction was written in 1984. For most computer science collections in larger public libraries. (RGK)

Directory of special libraries and information centers. Volumes 1 and 2. 9th ed. Edited by Brigitte T. Darnay. Detroit: Gale Research; 1985. Volume 1: 1735p. in two parts. $320.00 ISBN 0-8103-1888-1. Volume 2: 876p. $265.00. ISBN 0-8103-1889-X.

This is a new edition of a comprehensive guide to information centers, archives, and special and research libraries in the United States and Canada. Seventeen thousand, four hundred and sixty seven entries are given in Volume 1. Up to 25 points of information are provided for each entry. Included are seven appendixes such as networks and consortia, libraries for the handicapped, and patent depository libraries. There is a 3,000-term index to highly specific collection topics. Volume 2 contains two separate indexes: geographic and personnel. (Note: There is a Volume 3 called *New special libraries* which supplements Volumes 1 and 2 with up-to-date information between the ninth and tenth editions of the parent directory.) For virtually all special, university and larger public libraries. (RGK)

Government research directory. 3d ed. Edited by Kay Gill. Detroit: Gale Research; 1985. 675p. $325.00. ISBN 0-8103-0463-5.

This new edition of the guide contains 2302 U.S. Government organizations which conduct research programs. Two indexes provide access to the main body: name and keyword index and geographic index. Though expensive and in danger of become outdated rapidly, it is still a worthwhile acquisition for any academic, industrial, business, and large public library. (RGK)

Scientific and technical organizations and agencies directories. Edited by Margaret Labash Young. Detroit: Gale Publishing Co.; 1985. 2 vols. $140.00 ISBN 0-8103-2100-9.

Consists of two large volumes in which there are listings of the features of nearly 12,000 organizations of a scientific or technical nature. The volumes are divided into thirteen chapters such as sci-tech membership groups, research centers, federal and state agencies, consulting firms, standards organizations, educational institutions and patent sources. Most entries provide the usual information, such as name and address of the organizations, size, fields of research and person in charge. Although agriculture, the life sciences, medicine and the social sciences are not included, the volumes give thorough coverage to the physical and earth sciences, all types of engineering and mathematics. The volumes are concluded with a large keyword/name index; some idea of its size may be gained by noting that there are at least nine columns alone devoted to listings or organizations whose entries relate to the environment. Should be very useful in sci-tech reference collections. (EM)

Subject Directory of Special Libraries and Information Centers. 9th ed. Edited by Brigitte T. Darnay. Detroit: Gale Research: 1985. 5 vols. ISBN 0-81-3-1890-3 (set) $625.00 (set) $145.00 individual volumes.

Serves as a subject directory to Gale's *Directory of Special Libraries and Information Centers,* ninth edition, which see. Sci-tech libraries are found chiefly in volume 5, whose emphasis is on science and technology, including agriculture, computer science, energy, environment/ conservation and food science. This volume contains nearly 4700 of the set's total of more than 17,500 entries, with science and technology the largest portion of the volume (over 3200 entries). Other volumes of interest include military and transportation (vol.1), information science (vol. 2) and health sciences, which is the sole subject contained in vol. 3 (nearly 3000 entries). Typical entries provide nearly two dozen facts about libraries and information centers, including name, address, name and title of person in charge as well as other professional personnel, collection size, key subjects collected, number of subscriptions, network/consortia memberships and services offered. Each volume contains two indexes, one for titles or names of the libraries and the other for the subjects collected, arranged by state within the subject to facilitate location of a particular library in a given geographical area. (EM)

EXTANT

Annual review of astronomy and astrophysics. Volume 23. Edited by Geoffrey Burbridge. Palo Alto, CA: Annual Reviews; 1985. 466p. $44.00. ISBN 0-8243-0923-5.

A collection of 13 contributions providing truly high standard reviews. Of considerable interest is a survey of recent developments concerning the Crab Nebula and observations on Big Bang nucleosynthesis. Literature coverage is, as usual, most extensive as is the subject index. (RGK)

Catalysis. Volume 7. London: The Royal Society of Chemistry; 1985. 196p. $87.00. ISBN 0-85186-584-4.

This is a review of literature published up to the end of 1983 covering six aspects of catalysis of interest to research institutions and industry alike. Over 1000 literature references are provided. For all serious chemistry collections. (RGK)

Current topics in Chinese science. Volume 3. New York: Gordon and Breach; 1984. Section A. Physics, 486p. $58.00. ISBN 0-677-40375-5. Section B. Chemistry, 563p. $68.00. ISBN 0-677-40385-2. Section C. Mathematics, 869p. $98.00. ISBN 0-677-40405-0. Section D. Biology, 496p. $60.00. ISBN 0-677-40415-8. Section E. Astronomy, (Not available for review.) Section F. Earth science, 889p. $96.00. ISBN 0-677-40435-2. Section G. Medical science, 287p. $95.00. ISBN 0-677-40455-7.

Current achievements in research in the basic sciences in China are published in two journals: *Science in China (Scientia Sinica)* and *Science Bulletin (Kexue Tongbao)*. many disciplines are covered in these journals and in this particular set (Volume 3) they are collected from the journals' 1983 volumes and arranged into seven subject areas as the sections (above) indicate. This program should greatly ease the efforts of those scientists keeping abreast of developments in particular areas of Chinese science. These reviews are published mainly in English with occasional contributions in major European languages. For comprehensive science collections in industry, academe, and major public libraries. (RGK)

Organic reaction mechanisms 1983. Edited by A. C. Knipe and W. E. Watts. New York: Wiley; 1985. 589p. $130.00. ISBN 0-471-90503-8.

This is an annual survey covering the literature dated December 1982 through November 1983, principally in the area of physical organic chemistry. Four thousand, one hundred forty nine literature citations are given. It is the nineteenth volume in the series and should be available for quick reference in all serious chemistry collections. (RGK)

SCI-TECH ONLINE

Ellen Nagle, Editor

NATIONAL ONLINE MEETING

The National Online Meeting, held in New York City in May 1986, attracted its usual share of attention among practitioners, theorists and vendors. There were 4,000 attendees, 159 exhibitors and some 80 authors of papers. Numerous sessions devoted to descriptions of products were also held.

One obvious topic of high interest this year was that of CD-ROM, the laser disks now available for such uses as back files of online products. While several speakers described CD-ROM products as just another software option, there is no doubt others in attendance gave them a higher value for future developments.

In her annual survey of the online industry Martha Williams pointed out that in 1984 relatively few companies were making large sums of money, with only four of them earning more than one million dollars per year. Most make far less, perhaps reflective of her findings that the average searcher used 25 different databases during the course of the year, thus spreading payments over a number of products. The CD-ROM products on the market now number more than 40, she reported.

Other sessions touched on such matters as education of end users, front end services and downloading practices.

© 1986 by The Haworth Press, Inc. All rights reserved.

DATABASE NEWS

De Haen Drug Data Now on DIALOG

Detailed information on drugs and drug studies is now available from *De Haen Drug Data* (File 267) in DIALOG. With four major subfiles covering four distinct aspects of drug information, this database contains standardized, structured reports on drugs. Information is abstracted from over 1200 major international biomedical journals, as well as from such secondary sources as *SCRIP, Inpharma, FDC Reports,* and *Current Contents*. Other source materials include abstracts and summaries of papers presented at international meetings and symposia. The database which is produced by Paul de Haen contains the following subfiles:

> *Drugs in Use*—Reports on both marketed and investigational drugs involved in clinical studies.
> *Drugs in Research*—Reports of investigational drugs involved in pre-clinical and clinical studies.
> *ADRIS (Adverse Drug Reactions & Interactions System*—Reports of adverse drug reactions and drug interactions of both investigational and marketed drugs.
> *Drugs in Prospect*—Reports of newly synthesized compounds exhibiting pharmacological activity.

These subfiles may be searched either separately or simultaneously. This database enables searchers to review measurable data from drug studies; to analyze adverse reactions; and to track drug studies related to specific diseases or patient characteristics.

Records in *De Haen* summarize the findings of source publications as measurable data arranged in tabular form. The abstract includes a description of the study as well as its purpose, and conclusions derived from the study. In addition to the standard bibliographic fields, several fields are available for searching the specialized data found in the file. For example, a drug may be searched by dosage, route, molecular formula, drugs with which it interacts, duration, adverse reactions, and manufacturer, as well as by generic and trade names and synonyms, class and usage status.

De Haen Drug Data contains approximately 80,000 records dating from 1980 to the present. The file is updated every two months with approximately 2500 new records. The price for using the database is $66 per connect hour. There is a charge of $.25 for a full record printed online; $30 for each record printed offline.

CAB Abstracts Added by BRS

BRS has recently announced the availability of *CAB Abstracts*. Described as the largest agricultural database in the world, the file contains nearly 1 million references to articles, books, conference proceedings, technical reports, theses and patents from throughout the world. Approximately 30% of the citations are from literature published in the United States; more than 50 languages are included in the database. Literature from and about developing countries is given particular attention due to CAB International's commitment to provide information to member countries, many of which are developing nations.

Subject areas covered by *CAB Abstracts* include: agricultural engineering, animal breeding and production, applied entomology, pesticides, insecticides and herbicides, crop production, dairy science, economics and rural sociology, forestry and forest products, horticultural production, human nutrition, plant breeding, plant diseases, parasitology, soils and fertilizers, veterinary medicine, and weed control. Over 80% of the records in the database contain abstracts written by scientists on the CAB staff.

DIALOG has announced a reload of *CAB Abstracts* on their system, providing new capabilities and search features.

BIOSIS PREVIEWS on Mead Data Central

Biosciences Information Service has announced that the 1980–1985 portion of *BIOSIS Previews* is available online from The Reference Service of Mead Data. The database contains the machine-readable version of *Biological Abstracts* and *Biological Abstracts/RRM*. The 1980–85 segment contains more than two million records and provides access to life science literature published worldwide in over 9000 life science and biomedical publications. Approximately 500,000 records will be added to the database each year.

AGRIBUSINESS U.S.A. Offered by DIALOG

A centralized resource for comprehensive information on the business aspects of agriculture is now available as File 581 from DIALOG. Provided by Pioneer Hi-Bred International, Inc., the database is designed for tracking U.S. and regional agribusiness data including company names, trade names, new product development, and government policies. More than 300 agribusiness trade journals and government documents are covered, providing information on such topics as: agricultural finance, agricultural marketing, crop and livestock production, agricultural companies, businesses, and organizations, government legislation and regulations, agricultural technology including biotechnology, animal health and agricultural chemistry, agricultural business leaders, agricultural statistics, and current news affecting local, national and world agriculture.

AGRIBUSINESS U.S.A. records feature key access points such as Standard Industrial Classification (SIC) codes, DUNS numbers, company names and locations, trade names, geographic names, named persons, descriptors, and abstracts. The full text of government reports is available from 1986 to the present.

The database which contains 20,000 records is updated every two weeks with 1500 new records. The price for searching File 581 is $96 per connect hour; $.50 for each record printed online, and $.60 for each offline record.

National Science Foundation Records Added to FEDRIP

A new subfile has been added to the *FEDRIP (Federal Research in Progress)* database by DIALOG. The subfile consists of summaries of 400 research projects funded by the Engineering Directorate of the National Science Foundation. *FEDRIP* provides access to information about federally-funded research projects in physical science, engineering, and life science. Data elements generally include a project description, title, principal investigator, sponsoring and performing organizations, and a summary.

SEARCH SYSTEM NEWS

BRS Announces OCLC Gateway Service

BRS is offering an OCLC gateway to those OCLC members who are also BRS users. The service provides access to more than 100 BRS databases from OCLC dedicated-line terminals. The gateway provides a low-cost telecommunications link to the BRS system. Searchers can use this service to switch conveniently between the OCLC Online Union Catalog and the BRS databases.

DIALOGLINK Evaluation Disk Announced

A special evaluation disk is available for DIALOG customers who wish to try DIALOGLINK, DIALOG's custom communications software package, before purchasing it. The evaluation disk contains both the DIALOGLINK *Communications Manager* and the *Account Manager*. The cost of the disk is $10; the price may be applied towards the purchase of the complete DIALOGLINK package. For more information, call DIALOG Marketing at 800-3-DIALOG.

PUBLICATIONS AND SEARCH AIDS

NLM Introduces GRATEFUL MED

The National Library of Medicine has unveiled a new front-end software package for accessing NLM's MEDLINE, MEDLINE backfiles, and CATLINE databases via a personal computer. This software, named GRATEFUL MED, is designed to simplify the search process for an untrained or novice user. Health professionals, scientists, and others with a need for medical information can use this package to search without having knowledge of NLM's ELHILL search system, controlled vocabulary, or database structure. Experienced searchers can use the expert mode to take advantage of time-saving features such as automatic login and downloading of citations.

SCI-TECH IN REVIEW

Karla Pearce and Giuliana Lavendel, Editors

SECURITY

Brand, Marvine, (ed.) *Security for libraries. People, collections, buildings*. Chicago: American Library Association, 1984.

This broad survey of security issues in libraries covers histories and trends, electronic and manual systems, and legal and procedural issues. A lengthy bibliography is divided into sections from Archives to Theft and mutilation. (KJP)

COMPUTERS SOFTWARE

Clark, Phillip M. *Microcomputer spreadsheet models for libraries. Preparing budgets, documents, statistical reports*. Chicago: American Library Association, 1985.

A useful introduction to spreadsheet applications on Visicalc or Supercalc, although second generation programs may also be used. The author begins with a discussion of the who, what and why of spreadsheets, then follows with thirty spreadsheet models and some "warm-up exercises." (KJP)

MANAGEMENT

Kotter, John P. How to win friends outside the chain of command. *Working Smart*. 3 (4); 8–9; 1986 April.

Have you ever had problems trying to manage people who work for someone else? Can you sell your idea to someone who doesn't have to go along with it? The author gives some helpful advice to use in those difficult situations. (KJP)

Lowe, Terry R. Eight ways to ruin a performance review. *Personnel Journal.* 65(1). 60–62; 1986 January.

In a short discussion the author describes the pitfalls of a task many of us dread: the performance appraisal. He also offers a few suggestions which may be helpful for avoiding these difficulties, although probably not enough to make it easy. A short bibliography is appended. (KJP)

MODERN INFORMATION UNITS

Raitt, D.I. Look—no paper! The library of tomorrow. *The Electronic Library.* 3(4); 276–289; 1985 October.

This article goes beyond the usual evocation of robotics and interactive video to a useful overview of expert systems, input, output and other technologies, and a few integrated systems. Very useful is the author's extensive bibliography. (KJP)

Scott, Melinda J. The information center: confusing definition or evolving roles. *Information Management Review.* 1(3); 47–53; 1986 Winter.

The new information center—focussed on end-user access to information—is described. A sample mission statement as well as a table comparing the traditional information center with the knowledge center of the future, give useful ideas for greater patron involvement in your sci-tech library. (KJP)

For Product Safety Concerns and Information please contact our EU
representative GPSR@taylorandfrancis.com
Taylor & Francis Verlag GmbH, Kaufingerstraße 24, 80331 München, Germany

www.ingramcontent.com/pod-product-compliance
Lightning Source LLC
Chambersburg PA
CBHW052128300426
44116CB00010B/1816